FREE Test Taking Tips DVD Offer

To help us better serve you, we have developed a Test Taking Tips DVD that we would like to give you for FREE. **This DVD covers world-class test taking tips that you can use to be even more successful when you are taking your test.**

All that we ask is that you email us your feedback about your study guide. Please let us know what you thought about it – whether that is good, bad or indifferent.

To get your **FREE Test Taking Tips DVD**, email freedvd@studyguideteam.com with "FREE DVD" in the subject line and the following information in the body of the email:

   a. The title of your study guide.

   b. Your product rating on a scale of 1-5, with 5 being the highest rating.

   c. Your feedback about the study guide. What did you think of it?

   d. Your full name and shipping address to send your free DVD.

If you have any questions or concerns, please don't hesitate to contact us at freedvd@studyguideteam.com.

Thanks again!

TOEFL Preparation Book 2020 and 2021

TOEFL iBT Prep Study Guide Covering All Sections (Reading, Listening, Speaking, and Writing) with Practice Test Questions [With Audio Links for Listening Section]

TPB Publishing

Interested in buying more than 10 copies of our product? Contact us about bulk discounts:
bulkorders@studyguideteam.com

ISBN 13: 9781628457643
ISBN 10: 1628457643

Table of Contents

Quick Overview

As you draw closer to taking your exam, effective preparation becomes more and more important. Thankfully, you have this study guide to help you get ready. Use this guide to help keep your studying on track and refer to it often.

This study guide contains several key sections that will help you be successful on your exam. The guide contains tips for what you should do the night before and the day of the test. Also included are test-taking tips. Knowing the right information is not always enough. Many well-prepared test takers struggle with exams. These tips will help equip you to accurately read, assess, and answer test questions.

A large part of the guide is devoted to showing you what content to expect on the exam and to helping you better understand that content. In this guide are practice test questions so that you can see how well you have grasped the content. Then, answer explanations are provided so that you can understand why you missed certain questions.

Don't try to cram the night before you take your exam. This is not a wise strategy for a few reasons. First, your retention of the information will be low. Your time would be better used by reviewing information you already know rather than trying to learn a lot of new information. Second, you will likely become stressed as you try to gain a large amount of knowledge in a short amount of time. Third, you will be depriving yourself of sleep. So be sure to go to bed at a reasonable time the night before. Being well-rested helps you focus and remain calm.

Be sure to eat a substantial breakfast the morning of the exam. If you are taking the exam in the afternoon, be sure to have a good lunch as well. Being hungry is distracting and can make it difficult to focus. You have hopefully spent lots of time preparing for the exam. Don't let an empty stomach get in the way of success!

When travelling to the testing center, leave earlier than needed. That way, you have a buffer in case you experience any delays. This will help you remain calm and will keep you from missing your appointment time at the testing center.

Be sure to pace yourself during the exam. Don't try to rush through the exam. There is no need to risk performing poorly on the exam just so you can leave the testing center early. Allow yourself to use all of the allotted time if needed.

Remain positive while taking the exam even if you feel like you are performing poorly. Thinking about the content you should have mastered will not help you perform better on the exam.

Once the exam is complete, take some time to relax. Even if you feel that you need to take the exam again, you will be well served by some down time before you begin studying again. It's often easier to convince yourself to study if you know that it will come with a reward!

Test-Taking Strategies

1. Predicting the Answer

When you feel confident in your preparation for a multiple-choice test, try predicting the answer before reading the answer choices. This is especially useful on questions that test objective factual knowledge. By predicting the answer before reading the available choices, you eliminate the possibility that you will be distracted or led astray by an incorrect answer choice. You will feel more confident in your selection if you read the question, predict the answer, and then find your prediction among the answer choices. After using this strategy, be sure to still read all of the answer choices carefully and completely. If you feel unprepared, you should not attempt to predict the answers. This would be a waste of time and an opportunity for your mind to wander in the wrong direction.

2. Reading the Whole Question

Too often, test takers scan a multiple-choice question, recognize a few familiar words, and immediately jump to the answer choices. Test authors are aware of this common impatience, and they will sometimes prey upon it. For instance, a test author might subtly turn the question into a negative, or he or she might redirect the focus of the question right at the end. The only way to avoid falling into these traps is to read the entirety of the question carefully before reading the answer choices.

3. Looking for Wrong Answers

Long and complicated multiple-choice questions can be intimidating. One way to simplify a difficult multiple-choice question is to eliminate all of the answer choices that are clearly wrong. In most sets of answers, there will be at least one selection that can be dismissed right away. If the test is administered on paper, the test taker could draw a line through it to indicate that it may be ignored; otherwise, the test taker will have to perform this operation mentally or on scratch paper. In either case, once the obviously incorrect answers have been eliminated, the remaining choices may be considered. Sometimes identifying the clearly wrong answers will give the test taker some information about the correct answer. For instance, if one of the remaining answer choices is a direct opposite of one of the eliminated answer choices, it may well be the correct answer. The opposite of obviously wrong is obviously right! Of course, this is not always the case. Some answers are obviously incorrect simply because they are irrelevant to the question being asked. Still, identifying and eliminating some incorrect answer choices is a good way to simplify a multiple-choice question.

4. Don't Overanalyze

Anxious test takers often overanalyze questions. When you are nervous, your brain will often run wild, causing you to make associations and discover clues that don't actually exist. If you feel that this may be a problem for you, do whatever you can to slow down during the test. Try taking a deep breath or counting to ten. As you read and consider the question, restrict yourself to the particular words used by the author. Avoid thought tangents about what the author *really* meant, or what he or she was *trying* to say. The only things that matter on a multiple-choice test are the words that are actually in the question. You must avoid reading too much into a multiple-choice question, or supposing that the writer meant something other than what he or she wrote.

5. No Need for Panic

It is wise to learn as many strategies as possible before taking a multiple-choice test, but it is likely that you will come across a few questions for which you simply don't know the answer. In this situation, avoid panicking. Because most multiple-choice tests include dozens of questions, the relative value of a single wrong answer is small. As much as possible, you should compartmentalize each question on a multiple-choice test. In other words, you should not allow your feelings about one question to affect your success on the others. When you find a question that you either don't understand or don't know how to answer, just take a deep breath and do your best. Read the entire question slowly and carefully. Try rephrasing the question a couple of different ways. Then, read all of the answer choices carefully. After eliminating obviously wrong answers, make a selection and move on to the next question.

6. Confusing Answer Choices

When working on a difficult multiple-choice question, there may be a tendency to focus on the answer choices that are the easiest to understand. Many people, whether consciously or not, gravitate to the answer choices that require the least concentration, knowledge, and memory. This is a mistake. When you come across an answer choice that is confusing, you should give it extra attention. A question might be confusing because you do not know the subject matter to which it refers. If this is the case, don't eliminate the answer before you have affirmatively settled on another. When you come across an answer choice of this type, set it aside as you look at the remaining choices. If you can confidently assert that one of the other choices is correct, you can leave the confusing answer aside. Otherwise, you will need to take a moment to try to better understand the confusing answer choice. Rephrasing is one way to tease out the sense of a confusing answer choice.

7. Your First Instinct

Many people struggle with multiple-choice tests because they overthink the questions. If you have studied sufficiently for the test, you should be prepared to trust your first instinct once you have carefully and completely read the question and all of the answer choices. There is a great deal of research suggesting that the mind can come to the correct conclusion very quickly once it has obtained all of the relevant information. At times, it may seem to you as if your intuition is working faster even than your reasoning mind. This may in fact be true. The knowledge you obtain while studying may be retrieved from your subconscious before you have a chance to work out the associations that support it. Verify your instinct by working out the reasons that it should be trusted.

8. Key Words

Many test takers struggle with multiple-choice questions because they have poor reading comprehension skills. Quickly reading and understanding a multiple-choice question requires a mixture of skill and experience. To help with this, try jotting down a few key words and phrases on a piece of scrap paper. Doing this concentrates the process of reading and forces the mind to weigh the relative importance of the question's parts. In selecting words and phrases to write down, the test taker thinks about the question more deeply and carefully. This is especially true for multiple-choice questions that are preceded by a long prompt.

9. Subtle Negatives

One of the oldest tricks in the multiple-choice test writer's book is to subtly reverse the meaning of a question with a word like *not* or *except*. If you are not paying attention to each word in the question, you can easily be led astray by this trick. For instance, a common question format is, "Which of the following is…?" Obviously, if the question instead is, "Which of the following is not…?," then the answer will be quite different. Even worse, the test makers are aware of the potential for this mistake and will include one answer choice that would be correct if the question were not negated or reversed. A test taker who misses the reversal will find what he or she believes to be a correct answer and will be so confident that he or she will fail to reread the question and discover the original error. The only way to avoid this is to practice a wide variety of multiple-choice questions and to pay close attention to each and every word.

10. Reading Every Answer Choice

It may seem obvious, but you should always read every one of the answer choices! Too many test takers fall into the habit of scanning the question and assuming that they understand the question because they recognize a few key words. From there, they pick the first answer choice that answers the question they believe they have read. Test takers who read all of the answer choices might discover that one of the latter answer choices is actually *more* correct. Moreover, reading all of the answer choices can remind you of facts related to the question that can help you arrive at the correct answer. Sometimes, a misstatement or incorrect detail in one of the latter answer choices will trigger your memory of the subject and will enable you to find the right answer. Failing to read all of the answer choices is like not reading all of the items on a restaurant menu: you might miss out on the perfect choice.

11. Spot the Hedges

One of the keys to success on multiple-choice tests is paying close attention to every word. This is never truer than with words like almost, most, some, and sometimes. These words are called "hedges" because they indicate that a statement is not totally true or not true in every place and time. An absolute statement will contain no hedges, but in many subjects, the answers are not always straightforward or absolute. There are always exceptions to the rules in these subjects. For this reason, you should favor those multiple-choice questions that contain hedging language. The presence of qualifying words indicates that the author is taking special care with his or her words, which is certainly important when composing the right answer. After all, there are many ways to be wrong, but there is only one way to be right! For this reason, it is wise to avoid answers that are absolute when taking a multiple-choice test. An absolute answer is one that says things are either all one way or all another. They often include words like *every*, *always*, *best*, and *never*. If you are taking a multiple-choice test in a subject that doesn't lend itself to absolute answers, be on your guard if you see any of these words.

12. Long Answers

In many subject areas, the answers are not simple. As already mentioned, the right answer often requires hedges. Another common feature of the answers to a complex or subjective question are qualifying clauses, which are groups of words that subtly modify the meaning of the sentence. If the question or answer choice describes a rule to which there are exceptions or the subject matter is complicated, ambiguous, or confusing, the correct answer will require many words in order to be expressed clearly and accurately. In essence, you should not be deterred by answer choices that seem excessively long. Oftentimes, the author of the text will not be able to write the correct answer without

offering some qualifications and modifications. Your job is to read the answer choices thoroughly and completely and to select the one that most accurately and precisely answers the question.

13. Restating to Understand

Sometimes, a question on a multiple-choice test is difficult not because of what it asks but because of how it is written. If this is the case, restate the question or answer choice in different words. This process serves a couple of important purposes. First, it forces you to concentrate on the core of the question. In order to rephrase the question accurately, you have to understand it well. Rephrasing the question will concentrate your mind on the key words and ideas. Second, it will present the information to your mind in a fresh way. This process may trigger your memory and render some useful scrap of information picked up while studying.

14. True Statements

Sometimes an answer choice will be true in itself, but it does not answer the question. This is one of the main reasons why it is essential to read the question carefully and completely before proceeding to the answer choices. Too often, test takers skip ahead to the answer choices and look for true statements. Having found one of these, they are content to select it without reference to the question above. Obviously, this provides an easy way for test makers to play tricks. The savvy test taker will always read the entire question before turning to the answer choices. Then, having settled on a correct answer choice, he or she will refer to the original question and ensure that the selected answer is relevant. The mistake of choosing a correct-but-irrelevant answer choice is especially common on questions related to specific pieces of objective knowledge. A prepared test taker will have a wealth of factual knowledge at his or her disposal, and should not be careless in its application.

15. No Patterns

One of the more dangerous ideas that circulates about multiple-choice tests is that the correct answers tend to fall into patterns. These erroneous ideas range from a belief that B and C are the most common right answers, to the idea that an unprepared test-taker should answer "A-B-A-C-A-D-A-B-A." It cannot be emphasized enough that pattern-seeking of this type is exactly the WRONG way to approach a multiple-choice test. To begin with, it is highly unlikely that the test maker will plot the correct answers according to some predetermined pattern. The questions are scrambled and delivered in a random order. Furthermore, even if the test maker was following a pattern in the assignation of correct answers, there is no reason why the test taker would know which pattern he or she was using. Any attempt to discern a pattern in the answer choices is a waste of time and a distraction from the real work of taking the test. A test taker would be much better served by extra preparation before the test than by reliance on a pattern in the answers.

FREE DVD OFFER

Don't forget that doing well on your exam includes both understanding the test content and understanding how to use what you know to do well on the test. We offer a completely FREE Test Taking Tips DVD that covers world class test taking tips that you can use to be even more successful when you are taking your test.

All that we ask is that you email us your feedback about your study guide. To get your **FREE Test Taking Tips DVD**, email freedvd@studyguideteam.com with "FREE DVD" in the subject line and the following information in the body of the email:

- The title of your study guide.
- Your product rating on a scale of 1-5, with 5 being the highest rating.
- Your feedback about the study guide. What did you think of it?
- Your full name and shipping address to send your free DVD.

Introduction to the TOEFL iBT

Function of the Test

The Test of English as a Foreign Language (TOEFL) internet Based Test (iBT) is an exam developed and administered by the Educational Testing Service (ETS) to measure test takers' ability to use and comprehend academic English at a university level. As such, the TOEFL iBT is a widely recognized English language credential for students planning to study in American colleges and universities, as well as in English language academic programs and institutions in over 130 countries. TOEFL scores may also be accepted by some immigration authorities for visas that require an English language proficiency component (policies vary by country and visa type).

According to ETS, over 30 million people have taken the TOEFL. Because of the diverse range of uses for a TOEFL iBT score, the exam is appropriate for a diverse range of test takers. In addition to providing credentials for school admissions and visa applications, TOEFL iBT scores may also be used for hiring criteria or simply for personal evaluation of language progress. (https://www.ets.org/toefl/ibt/about/)

Test Administration

The TOEFL iBT must be taken at an authorized ETS test center. Testing centers located around the world offer the TOEFL iBT more than 50 times a year. Test takers must preregister one week before the exam; walk-in registration is not permitted. Refer to the ETS TOEFL website for a list of local test centers and exam dates. (https://www.ets.org/toefl/ibt/register/centers_dates) Test takers are permitted to retake the exam as many times as they choose, but are limited to one test within a 12-day period.

On the day of the exam, test takers must present two valid forms of photo ID. Other personal belongings are not permitted in the testing room. Electronic devices like phones, cameras, and watches are prohibited, even during break time. Food and beverages may be accessed during break time, and longer breaks or extended access to snacks and drinks may be available for test takers in need of exam accommodations. The TOEFL iBT offers a variety of other accommodations for students with disabilities, such as screen magnification, sign language interpretation, and Braille or audio versions of the test. (https://www.ets.org/toefl/ibt/register/disabilities/accommodations)

Test Format

The TOEFL iBT consists of four sections: reading, listening, speaking, and writing. It is necessary to take the entire test at once (it is not possible to take specific sections of the test). One ten minute break is given after the reading and listening sections.

The type of questions, number of questions, and time limit varies between subjects:

Subject	Number of questions	Time
Reading	3-4 passages with 12-14 questions per passage	60-80 minutes
Listening	4-6 lectures with 6 questions per lecture 2-3 conversations with 5 questions per conversation	60-90 minutes
Speaking	6 questions 2 Independent Speaking tasks 2 Integrated Speaking tasks	~20 minutes Response time: Independent speaking: 45 seconds per question Integrated speaking: 60 seconds per question
Writing	2 questions 1 Integrated Writing task 1 Independent Writing task	Integrated writing: 20 minutes Independent writing: 30 minutes
Total test time: 4 hours		

Test content is based on academic English. Reading and listening passages come from college level textbooks or lectures. Conversations will be related to campus topics and school life. The listening, speaking, and writing sections all include listening components (lectures and/or conversations), and speakers may have accented English from North America, the UK, Australia, or New Zealand.

Because TOEFL iBT is internet based, it is administered via computer. Test takers will use a headset with a microphone to listen to test questions and record their responses. Writing responses must be typed. (https://www.ets.org/toefl/ibt/faq/)

Scoring

Test takers can check their scores via their TOEFL online account approximately 10 days after completing the exam. Each section of the test is scored between 0-30 points, with a cumulative score of 0–120 points. Scores are valid for two years, and test takers are able to choose which valid scores from the past two years they wish to report to score recipients (although test scores must be used in their entirety; it is not possible to combine section scores from different test dates).

There are no "passing" or "failing" scores; rather, each institution or program determines its own guidelines for evaluating scores. According to data from 2015 exams, the average TOEFL iBT score is approximately 80 points. (https://www.ets.org/s/toefl/pdf/94227_unlweb.pdf) Many institutions look for scores at or above 80-90 points, while competitive programs may require scores of 100 points or higher (http://www.msinus.com/content/toefl-cut-off-score-323/). Requirements vary greatly; refer to each institution for their evaluation criteria.

Recent/Future Developments

The TOEFL iBT is the newest version of the test. Previously, TOEFL was a paper based test (PBT). The TOEFL PBT may still be administered in areas without reliable internet connection. Unlike the TOEFL iBT, the TOEFL PBT has no speaking section and only requires one essay response on the writing section. (https://www.ets.org/toefl/pbt/about/content/)

Study Prep Plan for the TOEFL iBT Exam

1 **Schedule -** Use one of our study schedules below or come up with one of your own.

2 **Relax -** Test anxiety can hurt even the best students. There are many ways to reduce stress. Find the one that works best for you.

3 **Execute -** Once you have a good plan in place, be sure to stick to it.

One Week Study Schedule		
Day 1	Reading	
Day 2	Listening	
Day 3	Speaking	
Day 4	Writing	
Day 5	Practice Questions	
Day 6	Essay	
Day 7	Take Your Exam!	

Two Week Study Schedule			
Day 1	Analysis of Science Excerpts	Day 8	Practice, but Don't Memorize
Day 2	Reading Strategies	Day 9	Organize
Day 3	Literary Elements	Day 10	Tell a Story
Day 4	Figurative Language	Day 11	Practice Questions
Day 5	Practice Questions	Day 12	Writing
Day 6	Listening	Day 13	Essay
Day 7	Practice Questions	Day 14	Take Your Exam!

	One Month Study Schedule					
Day 1	Analysis of History/ Social Studies Excerpts	Day 11	Recognizing the Structure of Texts	Day 21	Listen and Read the Questions Carefully
Day 2	Analysis of Science Excerpts	Day 12	Literary Elements	Day 22	Organize
Day 3	Reading Strategies	Day 13	Development of Themes	Day 23	Speak Clearly and Simply
Day 4	Main Idea	Day 14	Characteristics of Literary Genres	Day 24	Make Speech Slow
Day 5	Supporting Details	Day 15	Major Forms Within Each Genre	Day 25	Structure the Answer
Day 6	Analyzing Nuances of Word Meaning and Figures of Speech	Day 16	Figurative Language	Day 26	Practice Questions
Day 7	Meaning of Words in Context	Day 17	Practice Questions	Day 27	Writing
Day 8	Transitional Words and Phrases	Day 18	Listening	Day 28	First Essay
Day 9	Author's Use of Evidence to Support Claims	Day 19	Practice Questions	Day 29	Second Essay
Day 10	Making Logical Inferences	Day 20	Practice, but Don't Memorize	Day 30	Take Your Exam!

Reading

The Reading section is the first section on the TOEFL iBT® and is designed to assess the test taker's ability to understand university-level academic texts. The section includes 3-4 passages, with approximately 10-14 questions pertaining to each passage, for a total of 34-56 questions. The total allotted time for the Reading section ranges from 60-80 minutes. These ranges exist because Educational Testing Service (ETS) sometimes includes additional questions in the Reading section that enable test developers to assess the viability of potential future scored questions or to compare outcomes of various administrations of the TOEFL across the country, as benchmark questions. While test takers are not alerted to which test questions fall under either of these conditions, the experimental questions are unscored and as such, they do not affect one's results either way.

Each passage and its associated question is timed separately and given 20 minutes, so test takers with three passages test for an hour and those with four passages will have a Reading section that lasts 80 minutes. It should be noted that the questions pertaining to the passage will not appear on the computer screen until the test taker has scrolled all the way to the end of the passage. At that point, the passage text moves to the right side of the screen and the associated questions are listed on left. The passage questions do not need to be answered in order and test takers can skim them and then refer back to the passage to determine the correct answer.

Each passage is approximately 700 words and comes from an introductory-level university course text from any number of subjects such as biology, sociology, business, and literature. Test takers do not need prior experience or knowledge of the subject to answer the questions successfully; all necessary information is contained within the passages themselves. The test taker only needs to demonstrate his or her ability to comprehend academic texts, rather than convey an advanced understanding of the specific subject matter.

Test takers should be prepared to critically analyze the point of view and structure of the passage, as there are often multiple perspectives presented, and typically at least one question per passage addresses the organizational structure of the reading exercise.

The questions in the Reading section are of three possible formats, but each passage will have at least one question of each type:

- Multiple-choice questions with four answer options, in which the test taker selects the single best choice.

- Multiple-choice questions that present a sentence in the question and then display four answer options, each which denotes a specific area within the text of the passage. Test takers must select the single best choice that correctly indicates the point in the passage where the new sentence should be inserted.

- "Reading to Learn" questions, which list more than four choices and have more than one correct response and ask test takers to sort the provided answers into gaps in a provided chart or summary statement. Such questions assess the test taker's ability to decode the text's structure or to link ideas from various parts of the passage together.

The first type of multiple-choice questions can address a variety of things. These questions may require that the test taker identify the passage's or main idea or specific factual details that were explicitly stated in the text. Similarly, there are some questions in which the test taker must select the one detail that was *not* in the passage or is incorrectly presented in the answer choice in one way or another. Other questions may ask readers to identify the purpose of the passage in general or of specific statements, such that test takers need to decide *why* the author included a particular point. Some questions pull an entire sentence from the passage and then appear to simplify or paraphrase it in each of the four choice; incorrect choices will either omit important information from the original sentence or contain inaccurate details. Lastly, test takers may need to make logical inferences based on the passage or to determine the meaning of vocabulary words or pronouns referenced in the reading.

Analysis of History/Social Studies Excerpts

The TOEFL iBT® Reading section may include historically-based excerpts. The test may also include one or more passages from social sciences such as economics, psychology, or sociology.

For these types of questions, the test taker will need to utilize all the reading comprehension skills discussed below, but mastery of further skills will help. This section addresses those skills.

Comprehending Test Questions Prior to Reading

While preparing for a historical passage on a standardized test, first read the test questions, and then quickly scan the test answers prior to reading the passage itself. Notice there is a difference between the terms **read** and **scan.** Reading involves full concentration while addressing every word. Scanning involves quickly glancing at text in chunks, noting important dates, words, and ideas along the way. Reading test questions will help the test taker know what information to focus on in the historical passage. Scanning answers will help the test taker focus on possible answer options while reading the passage.

When reading standardized test questions that address historical passages, be sure to clearly understand what each question is asking. Is a question asking about vocabulary? Is another asking for the test taker to find a specific historical fact? Do any of the questions require the test taker to draw conclusions, identify an author's topic, tone, or position? Knowing what content to address will help the test taker focus on the information they will be asked about later. However, the test taker should approach this reading comprehension technique with some caution. It is tempting to only look for the right answers within any given passage. Do not put on "reading blinders" and ignore all other information presented in a passage. It is important to fully read every passage and not just scan it. Strictly looking for what may be the right answers to test questions can cause the test taker to ignore important contextual clues that actually require critical thinking in order to identify correct answers. Scanning a passage for what appears to be wrong answers can have a similar result.

When reading test questions prior to tackling a historical passage, be sure to understand what skills the test is assessing, and then fully read the related passage with those skills in mind. Focus on every word in both the test questions and the passage itself. Read with a critical eye and a logical mind.

Reading for Factual Information

Standardized test questions that ask for factual information are usually straightforward. These types of questions will either ask the test taker to confirm a fact by choosing a correct answer, or to select a correct answer based on a negative fact question.

For example, the test taker may encounter a passage from Lincoln's Gettysburg address. A corresponding test question may ask the following:

> Which war is Abraham Lincoln referring to in the following passage?: "Now we are engaged in a great civil war, testing whether that nation, or any nation so conceived and so dedicated, can long endure."

This type of question is asking the test taker to confirm a simple fact. Given options such as World War I, the War of Spanish Succession, World War II, and the American Civil War, the test taker should be able to correctly identify the American Civil War based on the words "civil war" within the passage itself, and, hopefully, through general knowledge. In this case, reading the test question and scanning answer options ahead of reading the Gettysburg address would help quickly identify the correct answer. Similarly, a test taker may be asked to confirm a historical fact based on a negative fact question. For example, a passage's corresponding test question may ask the following:

> Which option is incorrect based on the above passage?

Given a variety of choices speaking about which war Abraham Lincoln was addressing, the test taker would need to eliminate all correct answers pertaining to the American Civil War and choose the answer choice referencing a different war. In other words, the correct answer is the one that contradicts the information in the passage.

It is important to remember that reading for factual information is straightforward. The test taker must distinguish fact from bias. Factual statements can be proven or disproven independent of the author and from a variety of other sources. Remember, successfully answering questions regarding factual information may require the test taker to re-read the passage, as these types of questions test for attention to detail.

Reading for Tone, Message, and Effect

The Reading section does not just address a test taker's ability to find facts within a reading passage; it also determines a reader's ability to determine an author's viewpoint through the use of tone, message, and overall effect. This type of reading comprehension requires inference skills, deductive reasoning skills, the ability to draw logical conclusions, and overall critical thinking skills. Reading for factual information is straightforward. Reading for an author's tone, message, and overall effect is not. It's key to read carefully when asked test questions that address a test taker's ability to these writing devices. These are not questions that can be easily answered by quickly scanning for the right information.

Tone

An author's **tone** is the use of particular words, phrases, and writing style to convey an overall meaning. Tone expresses the author's attitude towards a particular topic. For example, a historical reading passage may begin like the following:

> The presidential election of 1960 ushered in a new era, a new Camelot, a new phase of forward thinking in U.S. politics that embraced brash action, unrest, and responded with admirable leadership.

From this opening statement, a reader can draw some conclusions about the author's attitude towards President John F. Kennedy. Furthermore, the reader can make additional, educated guesses about the state of the Union during the 1960 presidential election. By close reading, the test taker can determine that the repeated use of the word *new* and words such as *admirable leadership* indicate the author's tone of admiration regarding the President's boldness. In addition, the author assesses that the era during President Kennedy's administration was problematic through the use of the words *brash action* and *unrest.* Therefore, if a test taker encountered a test question asking about the author's use of tone and their assessment of the Kennedy administration, the test taker should be able to identify an answer indicating admiration. Similarly, if asked about the state of the Union during the 1960s, a test taker should be able to correctly identify an answer indicating political unrest.

When identifying an author's tone, the following list of words may be helpful. This is not an inclusive list. Generally, parts of speech that indicate attitude will also indicate tone:

- Comical
- Angry
- Ambivalent
- Scary
- Lyrical
- Matter-of-fact
- Judgmental
- Sarcastic
- Malicious
- Objective
- Pessimistic
- Patronizing
- Gloomy
- Instructional
- Satirical
- Formal
- Casual

Message

An author's **message** is the same as the overall meaning of a passage. It is the main idea, or the main concept the author wishes to convey. An author's message may be stated outright or it may be implied. Regardless, the test taker will need to use careful reading skills to identify an author's message or purpose.

Often, the message of a particular passage can be determined by thinking about why the author wrote the information. Many historical passages are written to inform and to teach readers established, factual information. However, many historical works are also written to convey biased ideas to readers. Gleaning bias from an author's message in a historical passage can be difficult, especially if the reader is presented with a variety of established facts as well. Readers tend to accept historical writing as factual. This is not always the case. Any discerning reader who has tackled historical information on topics such as United States political party agendas can attest that two or more works on the same topic may have completely different messages supporting or refuting the value of the identical policies. Therefore, it is important to critically assess an author's message separate from factual information. One author, for example, may point to the rise of unorthodox political candidates in an election year based on the failures of the political party in office while another may point to the rise of the same candidates in the same election year based on the current party's successes. The historical facts of what has occurred leading up to an election year are not in refute. Labeling those facts as a failure or a success is a bias within an author's overall message, as is excluding factual information in order to further a particular

point. In a standardized testing situation, a reader must be able to critically assess what the author is trying to say separate from the historical facts that surround their message.

Using the example of Lincoln's Gettysburg Address, a test question may ask the following:

> What is the message the author is trying to convey through this address?

Then they will ask the test taker to select an answer that best expresses Lincoln's message to his audience. Based on the options given, a test taker should be able to select the answer expressing the idea that Lincoln's audience should recognize the efforts of those who died in the war as a sacrifice to preserving human equality and self-government.

Effect

The **effect** an author wants to convey is when an author wants to impart a particular mood in their message. An author may want to challenge a reader's intellect, inspire imagination, or spur emotion. An author may present information to appeal to a physical, aesthetic, or transformational sense. Take the following text as an example:

> In 1963, Martin Luther King stated "I have a dream." The gathering at the Lincoln Memorial was the beginning of the Civil Rights movement and, with its reference to the Emancipation Proclamation, Dr. King's words electrified those who wanted freedom and equality while rising from hatred and slavery. It was the beginning of radical change.

The test taker may be asked about the effect this statement might have on King's audience. Through careful reading of the passage, the test taker should be able to choose an answer that best identifies an effect of grabbing the audience's attention. The historical facts are in place: King made the speech in 1963 at the Lincoln Memorial, kicked off the civil rights movement, and referenced the Emancipation Proclamation. The words *electrified* and *radical change* indicate the effect the author wants the reader to understand as a result of King's speech. In this historical passage, facts are facts. However, the author's message goes above the facts to indicate the effect the message had on the audience and, in addition, the effect the event should have on the reader.

When reading historical passages, the test taker should perform due diligence in their awareness of the test questions and answers up front. From there, the test taker should carefully, and critically, read all historical excerpts with an eye for detail, tone, message (biased or unbiased), and effect. Being able to synthesize these skills will result in success in a standardized testing situation.

Analysis of Science Excerpts

The Reading section may include passages that address the fundamental concepts of Earth science, biology, chemistry, or other sciences. Again, prior knowledge of these subjects is not necessary to determine correct test answers; instead, the test taker's ability to comprehend the passages is key to success. When reading scientific excerpts, the test taker must be able to examine quantitative information, identify hypotheses, interpret data, and consider implications of the material they are presented with. It is helpful, at this point, to reference the above section on comprehending test questions prior to reading. The same rules apply: read questions and scan questions, along with their answers, prior to fully reading a passage. Be informed prior to approaching a scientific text. A test taker should know what they will be asked and how to apply their reading skills. In this section of the test, it is also likely that a test taker will encounter graphs and charts to assess their ability to interpret scientific data with an appropriate conclusion. This section will determine the skills necessary to address scientific data presented through identifying hypotheses, through reading and examining data, and through interpreting data representation passages.

Examine Hypotheses

When presented with fundamental, scientific concepts, it is important to read for understanding. The most basic skill in achieving this literacy is to understand the concept of hypothesis and moreover, to be able to identify it in a particular passage. A **hypothesis** is a proposed idea that needs further investigation in order to be proven true or false. While it can be considered an educated guess, a hypothesis goes more in depth in its attempt to explain something that is not currently accepted within scientific theory. It requires further experimentation and data gathering to test its validity and is subject to change, based on scientifically conducted test results. Being able to read a science passage and understand its main purpose, including any hypotheses, helps the test taker understand data-driven evidence. It helps the test taker to be able to correctly answer questions about the science excerpt they are asked to read.

When reading to identify a hypothesis, a test taker should ask, "What is the passage trying to establish? What is the passage's main idea? What evidence does the passage contain that either supports or refutes this idea?" Asking oneself these questions will help identify a hypothesis. Additionally, hypotheses are logical statements that are testable and use very precise language.

Review the following hypothesis example:

> Consuming excess sugar in the form of beverages has a greater impact on childhood obesity and subsequent weight gain than excessive sugar from food.

While this is likely a true statement, it is still only a conceptual idea in a text passage regarding sugar consumption in childhood obesity, unless the passage also contains tested data that either proves or disproves the statement. A test taker could expect the rest of the passage to cite data proving that children who drink empty calories and don't exercise will, in fact, be obese.

A hypothesis goes further in that, given its ability to be proven or disproven, it may result in further hypotheses that require extended research. For example, the hypothesis regarding sugar consumption in drinks, after undergoing rigorous testing, may lead scientists to state another hypothesis such as the following:

> Consuming excess sugar in the form of beverages as opposed to food items is a habit found in mostly sedentary children.

This new, working hypothesis further focuses not just on the source of an excess of calories, but tries an "educated guess" that empty caloric intake has a direct, subsequent impact on physical behavior.

When reading a science passage to determine its hypothesis, a test taker should look for a concept that attempts to explain a phenomenon, is testable, logical, precisely worded, and yields data-driven results. The test taker should scan the presented passage for any word or data-driven clues that will help identify the hypothesis, and then be able to correctly answer test questions regarding the hypothesis based on their critical thinking skills.

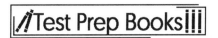

Reading Strategies

A **reading strategy** is the way a reader interacts with text in order to understand its meaning. It is a skill set that a reader brings to the reading. It employs a reader's ability to use prior knowledge when addressing literature and utilizes a set of methods in order to analyze text. A reading strategy is not simply tackling a text passage as it appears. It involves a more complex system of planning and thought during the reading experience. Current research indicates readers who utilize strategies and a variety of critical reading skills are better thinkers who glean more interpretive information from their reading. Consequently, they are more successful in their overall comprehension.

Pre-Reading Strategies

Pre-reading strategies are important, yet often overlooked. Non-critical readers will often begin reading without taking the time to review factors that will help them understand the text. Skipping pre-reading strategies may result in a reader having to re-address a text passage more times than is necessary. Some pre-reading strategies include the following:

- Previewing the text for clues
- Skimming the text for content
- Scanning for unfamiliar words in context
- Formulating questions on sight
- Recognizing needed prior knowledge

Before reading a text passage, a reader can enhance his or her ability to comprehend material by **previewing the text for clues**. This may mean making careful note of any titles, headings, graphics, notes, introductions, important summaries, and conclusions. It can involve a reader making physical notes regarding these elements or highlighting anything he or she thinks is important before reading. Often, a reader will be able to gain information just from these elements alone. Of course, close reading is required in order to fill in the details. A reader needs to be able to ask what he or she is reading about and what a passage is trying to say. The answers to these general questions can often be answered in previewing the text itself.

It's helpful to use pre-reading clues to determine the main idea and organization. First, any titles, sub-headings, chapter headings should be read, and the test taker should make note of the author's credentials if any are listed. It's important to deduce what these clues may indicate as it pertains to the focus of the text and how it's organized.

During pre-reading, readers should also take special note of how text features contribute to the central idea or thesis of the passage. Is there an index? Is there a glossary? What headings, footnotes, or other visuals are included and how do they relate to the details within the passage? Again, this is where any pre-reading notes come in handy, since a test taker should be able to relate supporting details to these textual features.

Next, a reader should **skim** the text for general ideas and content. This technique does not involve close reading; rather, it involves looking for important words within the passage itself. These words may have something to do with the author's theme. They may have to do with structure—for example, words such as *first, next, therefore,* and *last*. Skimming helps a reader understand the overall structure of a passage and, in turn, this helps him or her understand the author's theme or message.

From there, a reader should quickly **scan** the text for any unfamiliar words. When reading a print text, highlighting these words or making other marginal notation is helpful when going back to read text critically. A reader should look at the words surrounding any unfamiliar ones to see what contextual clues unfamiliar words carry. Being able to define unfamiliar terms through contextual meaning is a critical skill in reading comprehension.

A reader should also **formulate any questions** he or she might have before conducting close reading. Questions such as "What is the author trying to tell me?" or "Is the author trying to persuade my thinking?" are important to a reader's ability to engage critically with the text. Questions will focus a reader's attention on what is important in terms of ideas and supporting details.

Last, a reader should recognize that authors assume readers bring a prior knowledge set to the reading experience. Not all readers have the same experience, but authors seek to communicate with their readers. In turn, readers should strive to interact with the author of a particular passage by asking themselves what the passage demands they know during reading. If a passage is informational in nature, a reader should ask "What do I know about this topic from other experiences I've had or other works I've read?" If a reader can relate to the content, he or she will better understand it.

All of the above pre-reading strategies will help the reader prepare for a closer reading experience. They will engage a reader in active interaction with the text by helping to focus the reader's full attention on the details that he or she will encounter during the next round or two of critical, closer reading.

Strategies During Reading

After pre-reading, a test taker can employ a variety of other reading strategies while conducting one or more closer readings. These strategies include the following:

- Inferring the unspoken/unwritten text
- Clarifying during a close read
- Questioning during a close read
- Organizing the main ideas and supporting details
- Summarizing the text effectively

Inferring the unspoken or unwritten text demands the reader read between the lines in terms of an author's intent or message. The strategy asks that a reader not take everything he or she reads at face value, but instead, he or she will determine what the author is trying to say. A reader's ability to make inference relies on his or her ability to think clearly and logically about what he or she is reading. It does not ask that the reader make wild speculation or guess about the material but demands he or she be able to come to sound conclusion about the material, given the details provided and those not provided. A reader who can make logical inference from unstated text is achieving successful reading comprehension.

A reader needs to be able to **clarify** what he or she is reading. This strategy demands a reader think about how and what he or she is reading. This thinking should occur during and after the act of reading. For example, a reader may encounter one or more unfamiliar ideas during reading, then be asked to apply thoughts about those unfamiliar concepts after reading when answering test questions.

Questioning during a critical read is closely related to clarifying. A reader must be able to ask questions in general about what he or she is reading and questions regarding the author's supporting ideas. Questioning also involves a reader's ability to self-question. When closely reading a passage, it's not

enough to simply try and understand the author. A reader must consider critical thinking questions to ensure he or she is comprehending intent. It's advisable, when conducting a close read, to write out margin notes and questions during the experience. These questions can be addressed later in the thinking process after reading and during the phase where a reader addresses the test questions. A reader who is successful in reading comprehension will iteratively question what he or she reads, search text for clarification, then answer any questions that arise.

A reader should **organize** main ideas and supporting details cognitively as he or she reads, as it will help the reader understand the larger structure at work. The use of quick annotations or marks to indicate what the main idea is and how the details function to support it can be helpful. Understanding the structure of a text passage is sometimes critical to answering questions about an author's approach, theme, messages, and supporting detail. This strategy is most effective when reading informational or nonfiction text. Texts that try to convince readers of a particular idea, that present a theory, or that try to explain difficult concepts are easier to understand when a reader can identify the overarching structure at work.

Post-Reading Strategies

After completing a text, a reader should be able to **summarize** the author's theme and supporting details in order to fully understand the passage. Being able to effectively restate the author's message, sub-themes, and pertinent, supporting ideas will help a reader gain an advantage when addressing standardized test questions. Employing all of these strategies will lead to fuller, more insightful reading comprehension.

Main Idea

It is very important to know the difference between the topic and the main idea of the text. Even though these two are similar because they both present the central point of a text, they have distinctive differences. A **topic** is the subject of the text; it can usually be described in a one- to two-word phrase and appears in the simplest form. On the other hand, the **main idea** is more detailed and provides the author's central point of the text. It can be expressed through a complete sentence and can be found in the beginning, middle, or end of a paragraph. In most nonfiction books, the first sentence of the passage usually (but not always) states the main idea. Take a look at the passage below to review the topic versus the main idea.

Cheetahs *— ο TOPIC*

Cheetahs are one of the fastest mammals on land, reaching up to 70 miles an hour over short distances. Even though cheetahs can run as fast as 70 miles an hour, they usually only have to run half that speed to catch up with their choice of prey. Cheetahs cannot maintain a fast pace over long periods of time because they will overheat their bodies. After a chase, cheetahs need to rest for approximately 30 minutes prior to eating or returning to any other activity.

In the example above, the topic of the passage is "Cheetahs" simply because that is the subject of the text. The main idea of the text is "Cheetahs are one of the fastest mammals on land but can only maintain this fast pace for short distances." While it covers the topic, it is more detailed and refers to the text in its entirety. The text continues to provide additional details called **supporting details**, which will be discussed in the next section.

Supporting Details

Supporting details help readers better develop and understand the main idea. Supporting details answer questions like *who, what, where, when, why,* and *how*. Different types of supporting details include examples, facts and statistics, anecdotes, and sensory details.

Persuasive and informative texts often use supporting details. In persuasive texts, authors attempt to make readers agree with their point of view, and supporting details are often used as "selling points." If authors make a statement, they should support the statement with evidence in order to adequately persuade readers. Informative texts use supporting details such as examples and facts to inform readers. Take another look at the previous "Cheetahs" passage to find examples of supporting details.

Cheetahs

Cheetahs are one of the fastest mammals on land, reaching up to 70 miles an hour over short distances. Even though cheetahs can run as fast as 70 miles an hour, they usually only have to run half that speed to catch up with their choice of prey. Cheetahs cannot maintain a fast pace over long periods of time because they will overheat their bodies. After a chase, cheetahs need to rest for approximately 30 minutes prior to eating or returning to any other activity.

In the example above, supporting details include:

- Cheetahs reach up to 70 miles per hour over short distances.
- They usually only have to run half that speed to catch up with their prey.
- Cheetahs will overheat their bodies if they exert a high speed over longer distances.
- Cheetahs need to rest for 30 minutes after a chase.

Look at the diagram below (applying the cheetah example) to help determine the hierarchy of topic, main idea, and supporting details.

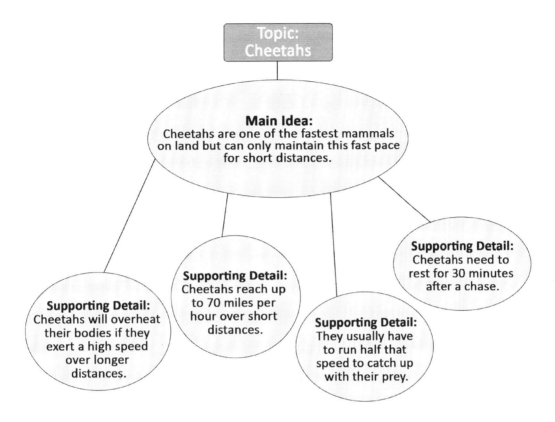

Analyzing Nuances of Word Meaning and Figures of Speech

Many words contain two levels of meaning: connotation and denotation. A word's **denotation** is its most literal meaning—the definition that can readily be found in the dictionary. A word's **connotation** includes all of its emotional and cultural associations.

In literary writing, authors rely heavily on connotative meaning to create mood and characterization. The following are two descriptions of a rainstorm:

- The rain slammed against the windowpane and the wind howled through the fireplace. A pair of hulking oaks next to the house cast eerie shadows as their branches trembled in the wind.

- The rain pattered against the windowpane and the wind whistled through the fireplace. A pair of stately oaks next to the house cast curious shadows as their branches swayed in the wind.

The first description paints a creepy picture for readers with strongly emotional words like *slammed*, connoting force and violence. *Howled* connotes pain or wildness, and *eerie* and *trembled* connote fear. Overall, the connotative language in this description serves to inspire fear and anxiety.

However, as can be seen in the second description, swapping out a few key words for those with different connotations completely changes the feeling of the passage. *Slammed* is replaced with the more cheerful *pattered*, and *hulking* has been swapped out for *stately*. Both words imply something large, but *hulking* is more intimidating whereas *stately* is more respectable. *Curious* and *swayed* seem more playful than the language used in the earlier description. Although both descriptions represent roughly the same situation, the nuances of the emotional language used throughout the passages create a very different sense for readers.

Selective choice of connotative language can also be extremely impactful in other forms of writing, such as editorials or persuasive texts. Through connotative language, writers reveal their biases and opinions while trying to inspire feelings and actions in readers:

- Parents won't stop complaining about standardized tests.
- Parents continue to raise concerns about standardized tests.

Readers should be able to identify the nuance in meaning between these two sentences. The first one carries a more negative feeling, implying that parents are being bothersome or whiny. Readers of the second sentence, though, might come away with the feeling that parents are concerned and involved in their children's education. Again, the aggregate of even subtle cues can combine to give a specific emotional impression to readers, so from an early age, students should be aware of how language can be used to influence readers' opinions.

Another form of non-literal expression can be found in **figures of speech**. As with connotative language, figures of speech tend to be shared within a cultural group and may be difficult to pick up on for learners outside of that group. In some cases, a figure of speech may be based on the literal denotation of the words it contains, but in other cases, a figure of speech is far removed from its literal meaning. A case in point is **irony**, where what is said is the exact opposite of what is meant:

> The new tax plan is poorly planned, based on faulty economic data, and unable to address the financial struggles of middle class families. Yet legislators remain committed to passing this brilliant proposal.

When the writer refers to the proposal as brilliant, the opposite is implied—the plan is "faulty" and "poorly planned." By using irony, the writer means that the proposal is anything but brilliant by using the word in a non-literal sense.

Another figure of speech is **hyperbole**—extreme exaggeration or overstatement. Statements like, "I love you to the moon and back" or "Let's be friends for a million years" utilize hyperbole to convey a greater depth of emotion, without literally committing oneself to space travel or a life of immortality.

Figures of speech may sometimes use one word in place of another. **Synecdoche**, for example, uses a part of something to refer to its whole. The expression "Don't hurt a hair on her head!" implies protecting more than just an individual hair, but rather her entire body. "The art teacher is training a class of Picassos" uses Picasso, one individual notable artist, to stand in for the entire category of talented artists. Another figure of speech using word replacement is **metonymy**, where a word is replaced with something closely associated to it. For example, news reports may use the word "Washington" to refer to the American government or "the crown" to refer to the British monarch.

Meaning of Words in Context

There will be many occasions in one's reading career in which an unknown word or a word with multiple meanings will pop up. There are ways of determining what these words or phrases mean that do not

require the use of the dictionary, which is especially helpful during a test where one may not be available. Even outside of the exam, knowing how to derive an understanding of a word via context clues will be a critical skill in the real world. The context is the circumstances in which a story or a passage is happening and can usually be found in the series of words directly before or directly after the word or phrase in question. The clues are the words that hint towards the meaning of the unknown word or phrase.

There may be questions that ask about the meaning of a particular word or phrase within a passage. There are a couple ways to approach these kinds of questions:

- Define the word or phrase in a way that is easy to comprehend (using context clues).
- Try out each answer choice in place of the word.

To demonstrate, here's an example from *Alice in Wonderland*:

> Alice was beginning to get very tired of sitting by her sister on the bank, and of having nothing to do: once or twice she <u>peeped</u> into the book her sister was reading, but it had no pictures or conversations in it, "and what is the use of a book," thought Alice, "without pictures or conversations?"

Q: As it is used in the selection, the word <u>peeped</u> means:

Using the first technique, before looking at the answers, define the word "peeped" using context clues and then find the matching answer. Then, analyze the entire passage in order to determine the meaning, not just the surrounding words.

To begin, imagine a blank where the word should be and put a synonym or definition there: "once or twice she _____ into the book her sister was reading." The context clue here is the book. It may be tempting to put "read" where the blank is, but notice the preposition word, "into." One does not read *into* a book, one simply reads a book, and since reading a book requires that it is seen with a pair of eyes, then "look" would make the most sense to put into the blank: "once or twice she <u>looked </u>into the book her sister was reading."

Once an easy-to-understand word or synonym has been supplanted, readers should check to make sure it makes sense with the rest of the passage. What happened after she looked into the book? She thought to herself how a book without pictures or conversations is useless. This situation in its entirety makes sense.

Now check the answer choices for a match:
   a. To make a high-pitched cry
   b. To smack
   c. To look curiously
   d. To pout

Since the word was already defined, Choice *C* is the best option.

Using the second technique, replace the figurative blank with each of the answer choices and determine which one is the most appropriate. Remember to look further into the passage to clarify that they work, because they could still make sense out of context.

a. Once or twice she <u>made a high pitched cry</u> into the book her sister was reading
b. Once or twice she <u>smacked</u> into the book her sister was reading
c. Once or twice she <u>looked curiously</u> into the book her sister was reading
d. Once or twice she <u>pouted</u> into the book her sister was reading

For Choice *A*, it does not make much sense in any context for a person to yell into a book, unless maybe something terrible has happened in the story. Given that afterward Alice thinks to herself how useless a book without pictures is, this option does not make sense within context.

For Choice *B*, smacking a book someone is reading may make sense if the rest of the passage indicates a reason for doing so. If Alice was angry or her sister had shoved it in her face, then maybe smacking the book would make sense within context. However, since whatever she does with the book causes her to think, "what is the use of a book without pictures or conversations?" then answer Choice *B* is not an appropriate answer. Answer Choice *C* fits well within context, given her subsequent thoughts on the matter. Answer Choice *D* does not make sense in context or grammatically, as people do not "pout into" things.

This is a simple example to illustrate the techniques outlined above. There may, however, be a question in which all of the definitions are correct and also make sense out of context, in which the appropriate context clues will really need to be honed in on in order to determine the correct answer. For example, here is another passage from *Alice in Wonderland*:

> . . . but when the Rabbit actually took a watch out of its waistcoat pocket, and looked at it, and then hurried on, Alice <u>started</u> to her feet, for it flashed across her mind that she had never before seen a rabbit with either a waistcoat-pocket or a watch to take out of it, and burning with curiosity, she ran across the field after it, and was just in time to see it pop down a large rabbit-hole under the hedge.

Q: As it is used in the passage, the word started means
a. To turn on
b. To begin
c. To move quickly
d. To be surprised

All of these words qualify as a definition of "start," but using context clues, the correct answer can be identified using one of the two techniques above. It's easy to see that one does not turn on, begin, or be surprised to one's feet. The selection also states that she "ran across the field after it," indicating that she was in a hurry. Therefore, to move quickly would make the most sense in this context.

The same strategies can be applied to vocabulary that may be completely unfamiliar. In this case, focus on the words before or after the unknown word in order to determine its definition. Take this sentence, for example:

> Sam was such a <u>miser</u> that he forced Andrew to pay him twelve cents for the candy, even though he had a large inheritance and he knew his friend was poor.

Unlike with assertion questions, for vocabulary questions, it may be necessary to apply some critical thinking skills that may not be explicitly stated within the passage. Think about the implications of the passage, or what the text is trying to say. With this example, it is important to realize that it is considered unusually stingy for a person to demand so little money from someone instead of just letting their friend have the candy, especially if this person is already wealthy. Hence, a <u>miser</u> is a greedy or stingy individual.

Questions about complex vocabulary may not be explicitly asked, but this is a useful skill to know. If there is an unfamiliar word while reading a passage and its definition goes unknown, it is possible to miss out on a critical message that could inhibit the ability to appropriately answer the questions. Practicing this technique in daily life will sharpen this ability to derive meanings from context clues with ease.

Transitional Words and Phrases

There are approximately 200 transitional words and phrases that are commonly used in the English language. Below are lists of common transition words and phrases used throughout transitions.

Time
- after
- before
- during
- in the middle

Example about to be Given
- for example
- in fact
- for instance

Compare
- likewise
- also

Contrast
- however
- yet
- but

Addition
- and
- also
- furthermore
- moreover

Logical Relationships
- if
- then
- therefore
- as a result
- since

Steps in a Process
- first
- second
- last

Transitional words and phrases are important writing devices because they connect sentences and paragraphs. Transitional words and phrases present logical order to writing and provide more coherent meaning to readers.

Transition words can be categorized based on the relationships they create between ideas:

- General order: signaling elaboration of an idea to emphasize a point—e.g., *for example, for instance, to demonstrate, including, such as, in other words, that is, in fact, also, furthermore, likewise, and, truly, so, surely, certainly, obviously, doubtless*

- Chronological order: referencing the time frame in which main event or idea occurs—e.g., *before, after, first, while, soon, shortly thereafter, meanwhile*

- Numerical order/order of importance: indicating that related ideas, supporting details, or events will be described in a sequence, possibly in order of importance—e.g., *first, second, also, finally, another, in addition, equally important, less importantly, most significantly, the main reason, last but not least*

- Spatial order: referring to the space and location of something or where things are located in relation to each other—e.g., *inside, outside, above, below, within, close, under, over, far, next to, adjacent to*

- Cause and effect order: signaling a causal relationship between events or ideas—e.g., *thus, therefore, since, resulted in, for this reason, as a result, consequently, hence, for, so*

- Compare and contrast order: identifying the similarities and differences between two or more objects, ideas, or lines of thought—e.g., *like, as, similarly, equally, just as, unlike, however, but, although, conversely, on the other hand, on the contrary*

- Summary order: indicating that a particular idea is coming to a close—e.g., *in conclusion, to sum up, in other words, ultimately, above all*

Author's Use of Evidence to Support Claims

Authors utilize a wide range of techniques to tell a story or communicate information. Readers should be familiar with the most common of these techniques. Techniques of writing are also commonly known as rhetorical devices; these are different ways of using evidence to support claims.

In non-fiction writing, authors employ argumentative techniques to present their opinion to readers in the most convincing way. First of all, persuasive writing usually includes at least one type of appeal: an appeal to logic (logos), emotion (pathos), or credibility and trustworthiness (ethos). When a writer appeals to logic, they are asking readers to agree with them based on research, evidence, and an established line of reasoning. An author's argument might also appeal to readers' emotions, perhaps by including personal stories and anecdotes (a short narrative of a specific event). A final type of appeal, appeal to authority, asks the reader to agree with the author's argument on the basis of their expertise or credentials. Consider three different approaches to arguing the same opinion:

Logic (Logos)
Below is an example of an appeal to logic. The author uses evidence to disprove the logic of the school's rule (the rule was supposed to reduce discipline problems; the number of problems has not been reduced; therefore, the rule is not working) and call for its repeal.

> Our school should abolish its current ban on cell phone use on campus. This rule was adopted last year as an attempt to reduce class disruptions and help students focus more on their lessons. However, since the rule was enacted, there has been no change in the number of disciplinary problems in class. Therefore, the rule is ineffective and should be done away with.

Emotion (Pathos)
An author's argument might also appeal to readers' emotions, perhaps by including personal stories and anecdotes.

The next example presents an appeal to emotion. By sharing the personal anecdote of one student and speaking about emotional topics like family relationships, the author invokes the reader's empathy in asking them to reconsider the school rule.

> Our school should abolish its current ban on cell phone use on campus. If they aren't able to use their phones during the school day, many students feel isolated from their loved ones. For example, last semester, one student's grandmother had a heart attack in the morning. However, because he couldn't use his cell phone, the student didn't know about his grandmother's condition until the end of the day—when she had already passed away, and it was too late to say goodbye. By preventing students from contacting their friends and family, our school is placing undue stress and anxiety on students.

Credibility (Ethos)
Finally, an appeal to authority includes a statement from a relevant expert. In this case, the author uses a doctor in the field of education to support the argument. All three examples begin from the same opinion—the school's phone ban needs to change—but rely on different argumentative styles to persuade the reader.

> Our school should abolish its current ban on cell phone use on campus. According to Dr. Bartholomew Everett, a leading educational expert, "Research studies show that cell phone usage has no real impact on student attentiveness. Rather, phones provide a valuable technological resource for learning. Schools need to learn how to integrate this new technology into their curriculum." Rather than banning phones altogether, our school should follow the advice of experts and allow students to use phones as part of their learning.

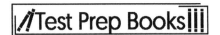

Making Logical Inferences

Critical readers should be able to make inferences. Making an **inference** requires the reader to read between the lines and look for what is *implied* rather than what is directly stated. That is, using information that *is* known from the text, the reader is able to make a logical assumption about information that is *not* directly stated but is probably true. Read the following passage:

"Hey, do you wanna meet my new puppy?" Jonathan asked.

"Oh, I'm sorry but please don't—" Jacinta began to protest, but before she could finish Jonathan had already opened the passenger side door of his car and a perfect white ball of fur came bouncing towards Jacinta.

"Isn't he the cutest?" beamed Jonathan.

"Yes—achoo!—he's pretty—aaaachooo!!—adora—aaa—aaaachoo!" Jacinta managed to say in between sneezes. "But if you don't mind, I—I—achoo!—need to go inside."

Which of the following can be inferred from Jacinta's reaction to the puppy?
   a. she hates animals
   b. she is allergic to dogs
   c. she prefers cats to dogs
   d. she is angry at Jonathan

An inference requires the reader to consider the information presented and then form their own idea about what is probably true. Based on the details in the passage, what is the best answer to the question? Important details to pay attention to include the tone of Jacinta's dialogue, which is overall polite and apologetic, as well as her reaction itself, which is a long string of sneezes. Answer Choices *A* and *D* both express strong emotions ("hates" and "angry") that are not evident in Jacinta's speech or actions. Answer Choice *C* mentions cats, but there is nothing in the passage to indicate Jacinta's feelings about cats. Answer Choice *B*, "she is allergic to dogs," is the most logical choice—based on the fact that she began sneezing as soon as a fluffy dog approached her, it makes sense to guess that Jacinta might be allergic to dogs. So even though Jacinta never directly states, "Sorry, I'm allergic to dogs!" using the clues in the passage, it is still reasonable to guess that this is true.

Making inferences is crucial for readers of literature because literary texts often avoid presenting complete and direct information to readers about characters' thoughts or feelings, or they present this information in an unclear way, leaving it up to the reader to interpret clues given in the text. In order to make inferences while reading, readers should ask themselves:

- What details are being presented in the text?
- Is there any important information that seems to be missing?
- Based on the information that the author *does* include, what else is probably true?
- Is this inference reasonable based on what is already known?

Recognizing the Structure of Texts in Various Formats

Writing can be classified under four passage types: narrative, expository, descriptive (sometimes called technical), and persuasive. Though these types are not mutually exclusive, one form tends to dominate the rest. By recognizing the *type* of passage you're reading, you gain insight into *how* you should read. If

you're reading a narrative, you can assume the author intends to entertain, which means you may skim the text without losing meaning. A technical document might require a close read, because skimming the passage might cause the reader to miss salient details.

1. **Narrative writing**, at its core, is the art of storytelling. For a narrative to exist, certain elements must be present. First, it must have characters While many characters are human, characters could be defined as anything that thinks, acts, and talks like a human. For example, many recent movies, such as *Lord of the Rings* and *The Chronicles of Narnia*, include animals, fantastical creatures, and even trees that behave like humans. Second, it must have a plot or sequence of events. Typically, those events follow a standard plot diagram, but recent trends start *in medias res* or in the middle (near the climax). In this instance, foreshadowing and flashbacks often fill in plot details. Finally, along with characters and a plot, there must also be conflict. Conflict is usually divided into two types: internal and external. Internal conflict indicates the character is in turmoil and is presented through the character's thoughts. External conflicts are visible. Types of external conflict include a person versus nature, another person, or society.

2. **Expository writing** is detached and to the point. Since expository writing is designed to instruct or inform, it usually involves directions and steps written in second person ("you" voice) and lacks any persuasive or narrative elements. Sequence words such as *first*, *second*, and *third*, or *in the first place*, *secondly*, and *lastly* are often given to add fluency and cohesion. Common examples of expository writing include instructor's lessons, cookbook recipes, and repair manuals.

3. Due to its empirical nature, **technical writing** is filled with steps, charts, graphs, data, and statistics. The goal of technical writing is to advance understanding in a field through the scientific method. Experts such as teachers, doctors, or mechanics use words unique to the profession in which they operate. These words, which often incorporate acronyms, are called **jargon**. Technical writing is a type of expository writing but is not meant to be understood by the general public. Instead, technical writers assume readers have received a formal education in a particular field of study and need no explanation as to what the jargon means. Imagine a doctor trying to understand a diagnostic reading for a car or a mechanic trying to interpret lab results. Only professionals with proper training will fully comprehend the text.

4. **Persuasive writing** is designed to change opinions and attitudes. The topic, stance, and arguments are found in the thesis, positioned near the end of the introduction. Later supporting paragraphs offer relevant quotations, paraphrases, and summaries from primary or secondary sources, which are then interpreted, analyzed, and evaluated. The goal of persuasive writers is not to stack quotes, but to develop original ideas by using sources as a starting point. Good persuasive writing makes powerful arguments with valid sources and thoughtful analysis. Poor persuasive writing is riddled with bias and logical fallacies. Sometimes logical and illogical arguments are sandwiched together in the same piece. Therefore, readers should display skepticism when reading persuasive arguments.

Literary Elements

There is no one, final definition of what literary elements are. They can be considered features or characteristics of fiction, but they are really more of a way that readers can unpack a text for the purpose of analysis and understanding the meaning. The elements contribute to a reader's literary interpretation of a passage as to how they function to convey the central message of a work. The most common literary elements used for analysis are presented below.

Point of View

The **point of view** is the position the narrator takes when telling the story in prose. If a narrator is incorporated in a drama, the point of view may vary; in poetry, point of view refers to the position the speaker in a poem takes.

First Person

The **first person point of view** is when the writer uses the word "I" in the text. Poetry often uses first person, e.g., William Wordsworth's "I Wandered Lonely as a Cloud." Two examples of prose written in first person are Suzanne Collins' *The Hunger Games* and Anthony Burgess's *A Clockwork Orange*.

Second Person

The **second person point of view** is when the writer uses the pronoun "you." It is not widely used in prose fiction, but as a technique, it has been used by writers such as William Faulkner in *Absalom, Absalom!* and Albert Camus in *The Fall*. It is more common in poetry—e.g., Pablo Neruda's "If You Forget Me."

Third Person

Third person point of view is when the writer utilizes pronouns such as *him, her*, or *them*. It may be the most utilized point of view in prose as it provides flexibility to an author and is the one with which readers are most familiar. There are two main types of third person used in fiction. **Third person omniscient** uses a narrator that is all-knowing, relating the story by conveying and interpreting thoughts/feelings of all characters. In **third person limited**, the narrator relates the story through the perspective of one character's thoughts/feelings, usually the main character.

Plot

The **plot** is what happens in the story. Plots may be singular, containing one problem, or they may be very complex, with many sub-plots. All plots have exposition, a conflict, a climax, and a resolution. The **conflict** drives the plot and is something that the reader expects to be resolved. The plot carries those events along until there is a resolution to the conflict.

Tone

The **tone** of a story reflects the author's attitude and opinion about the subject matter of the story or text. Tone can be expressed through word choice, imagery, figurative language, syntax, and other details. The emotion or mood the reader experiences relates back to the tone of the story. Some examples of possible tones are humorous, somber, sentimental, and ironic.

Setting

The **setting** is the time, place, or set of surroundings in which the story occurs. It includes time or time span, place(s), climates, geography—man-made or natural—or cultural environments. Emily Dickinson's poem "Because I could not stop for Death" has a simple setting—the narrator's symbolic ride with Death through town towards the local graveyard. Conversely, Leo Tolstoy's *War and Peace* encompasses numerous settings within settings in the areas affected by the Napoleonic Wars, spanning 1805 to 1812.

Characters

Characters are the story's figures that assume primary, secondary, or minor roles. Central or major characters are those integral to the story—the plot cannot be resolved without them. A central character can be a **protagonist** or hero. There may be more than one protagonist, and he/she doesn't always have to possess good characteristics. A character can also be an **antagonist**—the force against a protagonist.

Dynamic characters change over the course of the plot time. **Static** characters do not change. A **symbolic** character is one that represents an author's idea about society in general—e.g., Napoleon in Orwell's *Animal Farm*. **Stock** characters are those that appear across genres and embrace stereotypes—e.g., the cowboy of the Wild West or the blonde bombshell in a detective novel. A **flat** character is one that does not present a lot of complexity or depth, while a **rounded** character does. Sometimes, the **narrator** of a story or the **speaker** in a poem can be a character—e.g., Nick Carraway in F. Scott Fitzgerald's *The Great Gatsby* or the speaker in Robert Browning's "My Last Duchess." The narrator might also function as a character in prose, though not be part of the story—e.g., Charles Dickens' narrator of *A Christmas Carol*.

Development of Themes

Theme or Central Message

The **theme** is the central message of a fictional work, whether that work is structured as prose, drama, or poetry. It is the heart of what an author is trying to say to readers through the writing, and theme is largely conveyed through literary elements and techniques.

In literature, a theme can often be determined by considering the over-arching narrative conflict with the work. Though there are several types of conflicts and several potential themes within them, the following are the most common:

- **Individual against the self**—relevant to themes of self-awareness, internal struggles, pride, coming of age, facing reality, fate, free will, vanity, loss of innocence, loneliness, isolation, fulfillment, failure, and disillusionment

- **Individual against nature**—relevant to themes of knowledge vs. ignorance, nature as beauty, quest for discovery, self-preservation, chaos and order, circle of life, death, and destruction of beauty

- **Individual against society**—relevant to themes of power, beauty, good, evil, war, class struggle, totalitarianism, role of men/women, wealth, corruption, change vs. tradition, capitalism, destruction, heroism, injustice, and racism

- **Individual against another individual**—relevant to themes of hope, loss of love or hope, sacrifice, power, revenge, betrayal, and honor

For example, in Hawthorne's *The Scarlet Letter*, one possible narrative conflict could be the individual against the self, with a relevant theme of internal struggles. This theme is alluded to through characterization—Dimmesdale's moral struggle with his love for Hester and Hester's internal struggles with the truth and her daughter, Pearl. It's also alluded to through plot—Dimmesdale's suicide and Hester helping the very townspeople who initially condemned her.

Sometimes, a text can convey a **message** or **universal lesson**—a truth or insight that the reader infers from the text, based on analysis of the literary and/or poetic elements. This message is often presented as a statement. For example, a potential message in Shakespeare's *Hamlet* could be "Revenge is what ultimately drives the human soul." This message can be immediately determined through plot and characterization in numerous ways, but it can also be determined through the setting of Norway, which is bordering on war.

How Authors Develop Theme

Authors employ a variety of techniques to present a theme. They may compare or contrast characters, events, places, ideas, or historical or invented settings to speak thematically. They may use analogies, metaphors, similes, allusions, or other literary devices to convey the theme. An author's use of diction, syntax, and tone can also help convey the theme. Authors will often develop themes through the development of characters, use of the setting, repetition of ideas, use of symbols, and through contrasting value systems. Authors of both fiction and nonfiction genres will use a variety of these techniques to develop one or more themes.

Regardless of the literary genre, there are commonalities in how authors, playwrights, and poets develop themes or central ideas.

Authors often do research, the results of which contributes to theme. In prose fiction and drama, this research may include real historical information about the setting the author has chosen or include elements that make fictional characters, settings, and plots seem realistic to the reader. In nonfiction, research is critical since the information contained within this literature must be accurate and, moreover, accurately represented.

In fiction, authors present a narrative conflict that will contribute to the overall theme. In fiction, this conflict may involve the storyline itself and some trouble within characters that needs resolution. In nonfiction, this conflict may be an explanation or commentary on factual people and events.

Authors will sometimes use character motivation to convey theme, such as in the example from *Hamlet* regarding revenge. In fiction, the characters an author creates will think, speak, and act in ways that effectively convey the theme to readers. In nonfiction, the characters are factual, as in a biography, but authors pay particular attention to presenting those motivations to make them clear to readers.

Authors also use literary devices as a means of conveying theme. For example, the use of moon symbolism in Mary Shelley's *Frankenstein* is significant as its phases can be compared to the phases that the Creature undergoes as he struggles with his identity.

The selected point of view can also contribute to a work's theme. The use of first-person point of view in a fiction or non-fiction work engages the reader's response differently than third person point of view. The central idea or theme from a first-person narrative may differ from a third-person limited text.

In literary nonfiction, authors usually identify the purpose of their writing, which differs from fiction, where the general purpose is to entertain. The purpose of nonfiction is usually to inform, persuade, or entertain the audience. The stated purpose of a non-fiction text will drive how the central message or theme, if applicable, is presented.

Authors identify an audience for their writing, which is critical in shaping the theme of the work. For example, the audience for J.K. Rowling's *Harry Potter* series would be different than the audience for a biography of George Washington. The audience an author chooses to address is closely tied to the purpose of the work. The choice of an audience also drives the choice of language and level of diction an author uses. Ultimately, the intended audience determines the level to which that subject matter is presented and the complexity of the theme.

Characteristics of Literary Genres

Classifying literature involves an understanding of the concept of genre. A **genre** is a category of literature that possesses similarities in style and in characteristics. Based on form and structure, there are four basic genres.

Fictional Prose
Fictional prose consists of fictional works written in standard form with a natural flow of speech and without poetic structure. Fictional prose primarily utilizes grammatically complete sentences and a paragraph structure to convey its message.

Drama
Drama is fiction that is written to be performed in a variety of media, intended to be performed for an audience, and structured for that purpose. It might be composed using poetry or prose, often straddling the elements of both in what actors are expected to present. Action and dialogue are the tools used in drama to tell the story.

Poetry
Poetry is fiction in verse that has a unique focus on the rhythm of language and focuses on intensity of feeling. It is not an entire story, though it may tell one; it is compact in form and in function. Poetry can be considered as a poet's brief word picture for a reader. Poetic structure is primarily composed of lines and stanzas. Together, poetic structure and devices are the methods that poets use to lead readers to feeling an effect and, ultimately, to the interpretive message.

Literary Nonfiction
Literary nonfiction is prose writing that is based on current or past real events or real people and includes straightforward accounts as well as those that offer opinions on facts or factual events.

Major Forms Within Each Genre

Fictional Prose
Fiction written in prose can be further broken down into **fiction genres**—types of fiction. Some of the more common genres of fiction are as follows:

- **Classical fiction**: a work of fiction considered timeless in its message or theme, remaining noteworthy and meaningful over decades or centuries—e.g., Charlotte Brontë's *Jane Eyre*, Mark Twain's *Adventures of Huckleberry Finn*

- **Fables**: short fiction that generally features animals, fantastic creatures, or other forces within nature that assume human-like characters and has a moral lesson for the reader—e.g., *Aesop's Fables*

- **Fairy tales**: children's stories with magical characters in imaginary, enchanted lands, usually depicting a struggle between good and evil, a sub-genre of folklore—e.g., Hans Christian Anderson's *The Little Mermaid*, *Cinderella* by the Brothers Grimm

- **Fantasy**: fiction with magic or supernatural elements that cannot occur in the real world, sometimes involving medieval elements in language, usually includes some form of sorcery or witchcraft and sometimes set on a different world—e.g., J.R.R. Tolkien's *The Hobbit*, J.K. Rowling's *Harry Potter and the Sorcerer's Stone*, George R.R. Martin's *A Game of Thrones*

- **Folklore**: types of fiction passed down from oral tradition, stories indigenous to a particular region or culture, with a local flavor in tone, designed to help humans cope with their condition in life and validate cultural traditions, beliefs, and customs—e.g., William Laughead's *Paul Bunyan and The Blue Ox*, the Buddhist story of "The Banyan Deer"

- **Mythology**: closely related to folklore but more widespread, features mystical, otherworldly characters and addresses the basic question of why and how humans exist, relies heavily on allegory and features gods or heroes captured in some sort of struggle—e.g., Greek myths, Genesis I and II in the Bible, Arthurian legends

- **Science fiction**: fiction that uses the principle of extrapolation—loosely defined as a form of prediction—to imagine future realities and problems of the human experience—e.g., Robert Heinlein's *Stranger in a Strange Land*, Ayn Rand's *Anthem*, Isaac Asimov's *I, Robot*, Philip K. Dick's *Do Androids Dream of Electric Sheep?*

- **Short stories**: short works of prose fiction with fully-developed themes and characters, focused on mood, generally developed with a single plot, with a short period of time for settings—e.g., Edgar Allan Poe's "Fall of the House of Usher," Shirley Jackson's "The Lottery," Isaac Bashevis Singer's "Gimpel the Fool"

Drama

Drama refers to a form of literature written for the purpose of performance for an audience. Like prose fiction, drama has several genres. The following are the most common ones:

- **Comedy**: a humorous play designed to amuse and entertain, often with an emphasis on the common person's experience, generally resolved in a positive way—e.g., Richard Sheridan's *School for Scandal*, Shakespeare's *Taming of the Shrew*, Neil Simon's *The Odd Couple*

- **History**: a play based on recorded history where the fate of a nation or kingdom is at the core of the conflict—e.g., Christopher Marlowe's *Edward II*, Shakespeare's *King Richard III*, Arthur Miller's *The Crucible*

- **Tragedy**: a serious play that often involves the downfall of the protagonist. In modern tragedies, the protagonist is not necessarily in a position of power or authority—e.g., Jean Racine's *Phèdre*, Arthur Miller's *Death of a Salesman*, John Steinbeck's *Of Mice and Men*

- **Melodrama**: a play that emphasizes heightened emotion and sensationalism, generally with stereotypical characters in exaggerated or realistic situations and with moral polarization—e.g., Jean-Jacques Rousseau's *Pygmalion*

- **Tragi-comedy**: a play that has elements of both tragedy—a character experiencing a tragic loss—and comedy—the resolution is often positive with no clear distinctive mood for either—e.g., Shakespeare's *The Merchant of Venice*, Anton Chekhov's *The Cherry Orchard*

Poetry

The genre of **poetry** refers to literary works that focus on the expression of feelings and ideas through the use of structure and linguistic rhythm to create a desired effect.

Different poetic structures and devices are used to create the various major forms of poetry. Some of the most common forms are discussed in the following chart.

Type	Poetic Structure	Example
Ballad	A poem or song passed down orally which tells a story and in English tradition usually uses an ABAB or ABCB rhyme scheme	William Butler Yeats' "The Ballad of Father O'Hart"
Epic	A long poem from ancient oral tradition which narrates the story of a legendary or heroic protagonist	Homer's *The Odyssey* Virgil's *The Aeneid*
Haiku	A Japanese poem of three unrhymed lines with five, seven, and five syllables (in English) with nature as a common subject matter	Matsuo Bashō "An old silent pond . . . A frog jumps into the pond, splash! Silence again."
Limerick	A five-line poem written in an AABBA rhyme scheme, with a witty focus	From Edward Lear's *Book of Nonsense*: "There was a Young Person of Smyrna Whose grandmother threatened to burn her . . ."
Ode	A formal lyric poem that addresses and praises a person, place, thing, or idea	Edna St. Vincent Millay's "Ode to Silence"
Sonnet	A fourteen-line poem written in iambic pentameter	Shakespeare's Sonnets 18 and 130

Literary Nonfiction

Nonfiction works are best characterized by their subject matter, which must be factual and real, describing true life experiences. There are several common types of literary non-fiction.

Biography

A **biography** is a work written about a real person (historical or currently living). It involves factual accounts of the person's life, often in a re-telling of those events based on available, researched factual information. The re-telling and dialogue, especially if related within quotes, must be accurate and reflect reliable sources. A biography reflects the time and place in which the person lived, with the goal of creating an understanding of the person and his/her human experience. Examples of well-known biographies include *The Life of Samuel Johnson* by James Boswell and *Steve Jobs* by Walter Isaacson.

Autobiography

An **autobiography** is a factual account of a person's life written by that person. It may contain some or all of the same elements as a biography, but the author is the subject matter. An autobiography will be told in first person narrative. Examples of well-known autobiographies in literature include *Night* by Elie Wiesel and *Margaret Thatcher: The Autobiography* by Margaret Thatcher.

Memoir

A **memoir** is a historical account of a person's life and experiences written by one who has personal, intimate knowledge of the information. The line between memoir, autobiography, and biography is often muddled, but generally speaking, a memoir covers a specific timeline of events as opposed to the other forms of nonfiction. A memoir is less all-encompassing. It is also less formal in tone and tends to focus on the emotional aspect of the presented timeline of events. Some examples of memoirs in literature include *Angela's Ashes* by Frank McCourt and *All Creatures Great and Small* by James Herriot.

Journalism
Some forms of **journalism** can fall into the category of literary non-fiction—e.g., travel writing, nature writing, sports writing, the interview, and sometimes, the essay. Some examples include Elizabeth Kolbert's "The Lost World, in the Annals of Extinction series for *The New Yorker* and Gary Smith's "Ali and His Entourage" for *Sports Illustrated*.

Figurative Language

Whereas literal language is the author's use of precise words, proper meanings, definitions, and phrases that mean exactly what they say, **figurative language** deviates from precise meaning and word definition—often in conjunction with other familiar words and phrases—to paint a picture for the reader. Figurative language is less explicit and more open to reader interpretation.

Some examples of figurative language are included in the following graphic.

	Definition	Example
Simile	Compares two things using "like" or "as"	Her hair was like gold.
Metaphor	Compares two things as if they are the same	He was a giant teddy bear.
Idiom	Using words with predictable meanings to create a phrase with a different meaning	The world is your oyster.
Alliteration	Repeating the same beginning sound or letter in a phrase for emphasis	The busy baby babbled.
Personification	Attributing human characteristics to an object or an animal	The house glowered menacingly with a dark smile.
Foreshadowing	Giving an indication that something is going to happen later in the story	I wasn't aware at the time, but I would come to regret those words.
Symbolism	Using symbols to represent ideas and provide a different meaning	The ring represented the bond between us.
Onomatopoeia	Using words that imitate sound	The tire went off with a bang and a crunch.
Imagery	Appealing to the senses by using descriptive language	The sky was painted with red and pink and streaked with orange.
Hyperbole	Using exaggeration not meant to be taken literally	The girl weighed less than a feather.

Figurative language can be used to give additional insight into the theme or message of a text by moving beyond the usual and literal meaning of words and phrases. It can also be used to appeal to the senses of readers and create a more in-depth story.

Practice Questions

Fiction

Questions 1–10 are based on the following passage:

As long ago as 1860 it was the proper thing to be born at home. At present, so I am told, the high gods of medicine have decreed that the first cries of the young shall be uttered upon the anesthetic air of a hospital, preferably a fashionable one. So young Mr. and Mrs. Roger Button were fifty years ahead of style when they decided, one day in the summer of 1860, that their first baby should be born in a hospital. Whether this anachronism had any bearing upon the astonishing history I am about to set down will never be known.

I shall tell you what occurred, and let you judge for yourself.

The Roger Buttons held an enviable position, both social and financial, in ante-bellum Baltimore. They were related to the This Family and the That Family, which, as every Southerner knew, entitled them to membership in that enormous peerage which largely populated the Confederacy. This was their first experience with the charming old custom of having babies— Mr. Button was naturally nervous. He hoped it would be a boy so that he could be sent to Yale College in Connecticut, at which institution Mr. Button himself had been known for four years by the somewhat obvious nickname of "Cuff."

On the September morning consecrated to the enormous event he arose nervously at six o'clock, dressed himself, adjusted an impeccable stock, and hurried forth through the streets of Baltimore to the hospital, to determine whether the darkness of the night had borne in new life upon its bosom.

When he was approximately a hundred yards from the Maryland Private Hospital for Ladies and Gentlemen he saw Doctor Keene, the family physician, descending the front steps, rubbing his hands together with a washing movement—as all doctors are required to do by the unwritten ethics of their profession.

Mr. Roger Button, the president of Roger Button & Co., Wholesale Hardware, began to run toward Doctor Keene with much less dignity than was expected from a Southern gentleman of that picturesque period. "Doctor Keene!" he called. "Oh, Doctor Keene!"

The doctor heard him, faced around, and stood waiting, a curious expression settling on his harsh, medicinal face as Mr. Button drew near.

"What happened?" demanded Mr. Button, as he came up in a gasping rush. "What was it? How is she? A boy? Who is it? What—"

"Talk sense!" said Doctor Keene sharply. He appeared somewhat irritated.

"Is the child born?" begged Mr. Button.

Doctor Keene frowned. "Why, yes, I suppose so—after a fashion." Again he threw a curious glance at Mr. Button.

From *The Curious Case of Benjamin Button* by F.S. Fitzgerald, 1922.

1. According to the passage, what major event is about to happen in this story?
    a. Mr. Button is about to go to a funeral.
    b. Mr. Button's wife is about to have a baby.
    c. Mr. Button is getting ready to go to the doctor's office.
    d. Mr. Button is about to go shopping for new clothes.

2. What kind of tone does the above passage have?
    a. Nervous and Excited
    b. Sad and Angry
    c. Shameful and Confused
    d. Grateful and Joyous

3. As it is used in the fourth paragraph, the word *consecrated* most nearly means:
    a. Numbed
    b. Chained
    c. Dedicated
    d. Moved

4. What does the author mean to do by adding the following statement?

    "rubbing his hands together with a washing movement—as all doctors are required to do by the unwritten ethics of their profession."

    a. Suggesting that Mr. Button is tired of the doctor.
    b. Trying to explain the detail of the doctor's profession.
    c. Hinting to readers that the doctor is an unethical man.
    d. Giving readers a visual picture of what the doctor is doing.

5. Which of the following best describes the development of this passage?
    a. It starts in the middle of a narrative in order to transition smoothly to a conclusion.
    b. It is a chronological narrative from beginning to end.
    c. The sequence of events is backwards—we go from future events to past events.
    d. To introduce the setting of the story and its characters.

6. Which of the following is an example of an imperative sentence?
    a. "Oh, Doctor Keene!"
    b. "Talk sense!"
    c. "Is the child born?"
    d. "Why, yes, I suppose so—"

7. As it is used in the first paragraph, the word *anachronism* most nearly means:
    a. Comparison
    b. Misplacement
    c. Aberration
    d. Amelioration

8. This passage can best be described as what type of text?
    a. Expository
    b. Descriptive
    c. Narrative
    d. Persuasive

9. The main purpose of the first paragraph is:
    a. To explain the setting of the narrative and give information about the story.
    b. To present the thesis so that the audience can determine which points are valid later in the text.
    c. To introduce a counterargument so that the author can refute it in the next paragraph.
    d. To provide a description of the speaker's city and the building in which he works.

10. The end of the passage implies to the audience that:
    a. There is bad weather coming.
    b. The doctor thinks Mr. Button is annoying.
    c. The baby and the mother did not make it through labor.
    d. Something is unusual about the birth of the baby.

Social Science

Questions 11–20 are based on the following passage:

I heartily accept the motto, "that government is best which governs least," and I should like to see it acted up to more rapidly and systematically. Carried out, it finally amounts to this, which also I believe—"that government is best which governs not at all," and when men are prepared for it, that will be the kind of government which they will have. Government is at best but an expedient; but most governments are usually, and all governments are sometimes, inexpedient. The objections which have been brought against a standing army, and they are many and weighty, and deserve to prevail, may also at last be brought against a standing government. The standing army is only an arm of the standing government. The government itself, which is only the mode which the people have chosen to execute their will, is equally liable to be abused and perverted before the people can act through it. Witness the present Mexican war, the work of comparatively a few individuals using the standing government as their tool; for, in the outset, the people would not have consented to this measure.

This American government—what is it but a tradition, though a recent one, endeavoring to transmit itself unimpaired to posterity, but each instant losing some of its integrity? It has not the vitality and force of a single living man; for a single man can bend it to his will. It is a sort of wooden gun to the people themselves. But it is not the less necessary for this; for the people must have some complicated machinery or other, and hear its din, to satisfy that idea of government which they have. Governments show thus how successfully men can be imposed on, even impose on themselves, for their own advantage. It is excellent, we must all allow. Yet this government never of itself furthered any enterprise, but by the alacrity with which it got out of its way. It does not keep the country free. It does not settle the West. It does not educate. The character inherent in the American people has done all that has been accomplished; and it would have done somewhat more, if the government had not sometimes got in its way. For government is an expedient by which men would fain succeed in letting one another alone; and, as has been said, when it is most expedient, the governed are most let alone by it. Trade and commerce, if they were not made of India-rubber, would never manage to bounce over the obstacles which legislators are continually putting in their way; and, if one were to judge these men wholly by the effects of their actions and not partly by their intentions, they would deserve to be classed and punished with those mischievous persons who put obstructions on the railroads.

But, to speak practically and as a citizen, unlike those who call themselves no-government men, I ask for, not at once no government, but at once a better government. Let every man make known what kind of government would command his respect, and that will be one step toward obtaining it.

Excerpt from *Civil Disobedience* by Henry David Thoreau

11. Which phrase best encapsulates Thoreau's use of the term *expedient* in the first paragraph?
   a. A dead end
   b. A state of order
   c. A means to an end
   d. Rushed construction

12. Which best describes Thoreau's view on the Mexican War?
   a. Government is inherently corrupt because it must wage war.
   b. Government can easily be manipulated by a few individuals for their own agenda.
   c. Government is a tool for the people, but it can also act against their interest.
   d. The Mexican War was a necessary action, but not all the people believed this.

13. What is Thoreau's purpose for writing?
   a. His goal is to illustrate how government can function if ideals are maintained.
   b. He wants to prove that true democracy is the best government, but it can be corrupted easily.
   c. Thoreau reflects on the stages of government abuses.
   d. He is seeking to prove that government is easily corruptible and inherently restrictive of individual freedoms that can simultaneously affect the whole state.

14. Which example best supports Thoreau's argument?
   a. A vote carries in the Senate to create a new road tax.
   b. The president vetoes the new FARM bill.
   c. Prohibition is passed to outlaw alcohol.
   d. Trade is opened between the United States and Iceland.

15. Which best summarizes this section from the following passage?

"This American government—what is it but a tradition, though a recent one, endeavoring to transmit itself unimpaired to posterity, but each instant losing some of its integrity? It has not the vitality and force of a single living man; for a single man can bend it to his will. It is a sort of wooden gun to the people themselves."

a. The government may be instituted to ensure the protections of freedoms, but this is weakened by the fact that it is easily manipulated by individuals.
b. Unlike an individual, government is uncaring.
c. Unlike an individual, government has no will, making it more prone to be used as a weapon against the people.
d. American government is modeled after other traditions but actually has greater potential to be used to control people.

16. According to Thoreau, what's the main reason why government eventually fails to achieve progress?
a. There are too many rules.
b. Legislation eventually becomes a hindrance to the lives and work of everyday people.
c. Trade and wealth eventually become the driving factor of those in government.
d. Government doesn't separate religion and state.

17. What type of passage is this?
a. Narrative
b. Descriptive
c. Persuasive
d. Expository

18. As it is used in the first paragraph, the word *liable* most nearly means:
a. Paramount
b. Inconceivable
c. Susceptible
d. Detrimental

19. According to the passage, which government is Thoreau talking about?
a. Mexican
b. American
c. Chinese
d. British

20. As it is used in the second paragraph, the word *posterity* most nearly means:
a. Persons of royal lineage.
b. All future generations of people.
c. A person involved in directing education.
d. A person who offers views on important life questions

Humanities

Questions 21–30 are based on the following passage:

Four hundred years ago, in 1612, the north-west of England was the scene of England's biggest peacetime witch trial: the trial of the Lancashire witches. Twenty people, mostly from the Pendle area of Lancashire, were imprisoned in the castle as witches. Ten were hanged, one died in gaol, one was sentenced to stand in the pillory, and eight were acquitted. The 2012 anniversary sees a small flood of commemorative events, including works of fiction by Blake Morrison, Carol Ann Duffy, and Jeanette Winterson. How did this witch trial come about, and what accounts for its enduring fame?

We know so much about the Lancashire Witches because the trial was recorded in unique detail by the clerk of the court, Thomas Potts, who published his account soon afterwards as *The Wonderful Discovery of Witches in the County of Lancaster*. I have recently published a modern-English edition of this book, together with an essay piecing together what we know of the events of 1612. It has been a fascinating exercise, revealing how Potts carefully edited the evidence, and also how the case against the "witches" was constructed and manipulated to bring about a spectacular show trial. It all began in mid-March when a pedlar from Halifax named John Law had a frightening encounter with a poor young woman, Alizon Device, in a field near Colne. He refused her request for pins and there was a brief argument during which he was seized by a fit that left him with "his head … drawn awry, his eyes and face deformed, his speech not well to be understood; his thighs and legs stark lame." We can now recognize this as a stroke, perhaps triggered by the stressful encounter. Alizon Device was sent for and surprised all by confessing to the bewitching of John Law and then begged for forgiveness.

When Alizon Device was unable to cure the pedlar, the local magistrate, Roger Nowell was called in. Characterized by Thomas Potts as "God's justice" he was alert to instances of witchcraft, which were regarded by the Lancashire's puritan-inclined authorities as part of the cultural rubble of "popery"—Roman Catholicism—long overdue to be swept away at the end of the country's very slow protestant reformation. "With weeping tears" Alizon explained that she had been led astray by her grandmother, "old Demdike," well-known in the district for her knowledge of old Catholic prayers, charms, cures, magic, and curses. Nowell quickly interviewed Alizon's grandmother and mother, as well as Demdike's supposed rival, "old Chattox" and her daughter Anne. Their panicky attempts to explain themselves and shift the blame to others eventually only ended up incriminating them, and the four were sent to Lancaster gaol in early April to await trial at the summer assizes. The initial picture revealed was of a couple of poor, marginal local families in the forest of Pendle with a longstanding reputation for magical powers, which they had occasionally used at the request of their wealthier neighbours. There had been disputes but none of these were part of ordinary village life. Not until 1612 did any of this come to the attention of the authorities.

The net was widened still further at the end of April when Alizon's younger brother James and younger sister Jennet, only nine years old, came up between them with a story about a "great meeting of witches" at their grandmother's house, known as Malkin Tower. This meeting was presumably to discuss the plight of those arrested and the threat of further arrests, but according to the evidence extracted from the children by the magistrates, a plot was hatched to blow up Lancaster castle with gunpowder, kill the gaoler, and rescue the imprisoned witches. It was, in short, a conspiracy against royal authority to rival the gunpowder plot of 1605—

something to be expected in a county known for its particularly strong underground Roman Catholic presence.

Those present at the meeting were mostly family members and neighbours, but they also included Alice Nutter, described by Potts as "a rich woman [who] had a great estate, and children of good hope: in the common opinion of the world, of good temper, free from envy or malice." Her part in the affair remains mysterious, but she seems to have had Catholic family connections, and may have been one herself, providing an added motive for her to be prosecuted.

"The Lancashire Witches 1612–2012" by Robert Poole.

This article (The Lancaster Witches 1612-2012) was originally published in The Public Domain Review under a Creative Commons Attribution-ShareAlike 3.0. If you wish to reuse it, please see: http://publicdomainreview.org/legal/

21. What's the point of this passage, and why did the author write it?
a. The author is documenting a historic witchcraft trial while uncovering/investigating the role of suspicion and anti-Catholicism in the events.
b. The author seeks long-overdue reparations for the ancestors of those accused and executed for witchcraft in Lancashire.
c. The author is educating the reader about actual occult practices of the 1600s.
d. The author argues that the Lancashire witch trials were more brutal than the infamous Salem trials.

22. Which term best captures the meaning of the author's use of *enduring* in the first paragraph?
a. Un-original
b. Popular
c. Wicked
d. Circumstantial

23. What textual information is present within the passage that most lends itself to the author's credibility?
a. His prose is consistent with the time.
b. This is a reflective passage; the author doesn't need to establish credibility.
c. The author cites specific quotes.
d. The author has published a modern account of the case and has written on the subject before.

24. What might the following excerpt suggest about the trial or, at the very least, Thomas Potts' account of the trial(s)?

"It has been a fascinating exercise, revealing how Potts carefully edited the evidence, and also how the case against the 'witches' was constructed and manipulated to bring about a spectacular show trial."

a. The events were so grand that the public was allowed access to such a spectacular set of cases.
b. Sections may have been exaggerated or stretched to create notoriety on an extraordinary case.
c. Evidence was faked, making the trial a total farce.
d. The trial was corrupt from the beginning.

25. Which statement best describes the political atmosphere of the 1600s that influenced the Alizon Device witch trial/case?
    a. Fear of witches was prevalent during this period.
    b. Magistrates were seeking ways to cement their power during this period of unrest.
    c. In a highly superstitious culture, the Protestant church and government were highly motivated to root out any potential sources that could undermine the current regime.
    d. Lancashire was originally a prominent area for pagan celebration, making the modern Protestants very weary of whispers of witchcraft and open to witch trials to resolve any potential threats to Christianity.

26. Which best describes the strongest "evidence" used in the case against Alizon and the witches?
    a. Knowledge of the occult and witchcraft
    b. "Spectral evidence"
    c. Popular rumors of witchcraft and Catholic association
    d. Self-incriminating speech

27. What type of passage is this?
    a. Persuasive
    b. Expository
    c. Narrative
    d. Descriptive

28. According to the passage, how many people were arrested as witches in the Lancashire trials?
    a. 10
    b. 20
    c. 30
    d. 40

29. As it is used in the first paragraph, the word *commemorative* most nearly means:
    a. Associated with being acquitted
    b. An act of disloyalty
    c. A circumstance to be disliked
    d. In honor of something

30. According to the passage, what is Malkin tower?
    a. The building where the trial of the Lancashire witches took place.
    b. The grandmother's house of the peddler who sought revenge on Alizon.
    c. Alizon's grandmother's house where a meeting of witches was held.
    d. The residence of a jury member who witnessed the cursing of the peddler.

Natural Science

Questions 31–40 are based upon the following passage:

Insects as a whole are preeminently creatures of the land and the air. This is shown not only by the possession of wings by a vast majority of the class, but by the mode of breathing to which reference has already been made, a system of branching air-tubes carrying atmospheric air with its combustion-supporting oxygen to all the insect's tissues. The air gains access to these tubes through a number of paired air-holes or spiracles, arranged segmentally in series.

It is of great interest to find that, nevertheless, a number of insects spend much of their time under water. This is true of not a few in the perfect winged state, as for example aquatic beetles and water-bugs ('boatmen' and 'scorpions') which have some way of protecting their spiracles when submerged, and, possessing usually the power of flight, can pass on occasion from pond or stream to upper air. But it is advisable in connection with our present subject to dwell especially on some insects that remain continually under water till they are ready to undergo their final moult and attain the winged state, which they pass entirely in the air. The preparatory instars of such insects are aquatic; the adult instar is aerial. All may-flies, dragon-flies, and caddis-flies, many beetles and two-winged flies, and a few moths thus divide their life-story between the water and the air. For the present we confine attention to the Stone-flies, the May-flies, and the Dragon-flies, three well-known orders of insects respectively called by systematists the Plecoptera, the Ephemeroptera and the Odonata.

In the case of many insects that have aquatic larvae, the latter are provided with some arrangement for enabling them to reach atmospheric air through the surface-film of the water. But the larva of a stone-fly, a dragon-fly, or a may-fly is adapted more completely than these for aquatic life; it can, by means of gills of some kind, breathe the air dissolved in water.

This excerpt is from The Life-Story of Insects by Geo H. Carpenter

31. Which statement best details the central idea in this passage?
    a. It introduces certain insects that transition from water to air.
    b. It delves into entomology, especially where gills are concerned.
    c. It defines what constitutes as insects' breathing.
    d. It invites readers to have a hand in the preservation of insects.

32. Which definition most closely relates to the usage of the word *moult* in the passage?
    a. An adventure of sorts, especially underwater
    b. Mating act between two insects
    c. The act of shedding part or all of the outer shell
    d. Death of an organism that ends in a revival of life

33. What is the purpose of the first paragraph in relation to the second paragraph?
    a. The first paragraph serves as a cause and the second paragraph serves as an effect.
    b. The first paragraph serves as a contrast to the second.
    c. The first paragraph is a description for the argument in the second paragraph.
    d. The first and second paragraphs are merely presented in a sequence.

34. What does the following sentence most nearly mean?

The preparatory instars of such insects are aquatic; the adult instar is aerial.

a. The volume of water is necessary to prep the insect for transition rather than the volume of the air.
b. The abdomen of the insect is designed like a star in the water as well as the air.
c. The stage of preparation in between molting is acted out in the water, while the last stage is in the air.
d. These insects breathe first in the water through gills, yet continue to use the same organs to breathe in the air.

35. Which of the statements reflect information that one could reasonably infer based on the author's tone?
a. The author's tone is persuasive and attempts to call the audience to action.
b. The author's tone is passionate due to excitement over the subject and personal narrative.
c. The author's tone is informative and exhibits interest in the subject of the study.
d. The author's tone is somber, depicting some anger at the state of insect larvae.

36. Which statement best describes stoneflies, mayflies, and dragonflies?
a. They are creatures of the land and the air.
b. They have a way of protecting their spiracles when submerged.
c. Their larvae can breathe the air dissolved in water through gills of some kind.
d. The preparatory instars of these insects are aerial.

37. According to the passage, what is true of "boatmen" and "scorpions"?
a. They have no way of protecting their spiracles when submerged.
b. They have some way of protecting their spiracles when submerged.
c. They usually do not possess the power of flight.
d. They remain continually under water till they are ready to undergo their final moult.

38. The last paragraph indicates that the author believes
a. That the stonefly, dragonfly, and mayfly larvae are better prepared to live beneath the water because they have gills that allow them to do so.
b. That the stonefly is different from the mayfly because the stonefly can breathe underwater and the mayfly can only breathe above water.
c. That the dragonfly is a unique species in that its larvae lives mostly underwater for most of its young life.
d. That the stonefly larvae can breathe only by reaching the surface film of the water.

39. According to the passage, why are insects as a whole are preeminently creatures of the land and the air?
a. Because insects are born on land but eventually end up adapting to life underwater for the rest of their adult lives.
b. Because most insects have legs made for walking on land and tube-like structures on their bellies for skimming the water.
c. Because a vast majority of insects have wings and also have the ability to breathe underwater.
d. Because most insects have a propulsion method specifically designed for underwater use, but they can only breathe on land.

40. As it is used in the first paragraph, the word *preeminently* most nearly means:
    a. Unknowingly
    b. Above all
    c. Most truthfully
    d. Not importantly

Answer Explanations

1. B: Mr. Button's wife is about to have a baby. The passage begins by giving the reader information about traditional birthing situations. Then, we are told that Mr. and Mrs. Button decide to go against tradition to have their baby in a hospital. The next few passages are dedicated to letting the reader know how Mr. Button dresses and goes to the hospital to welcome his new baby. There is a doctor in this excerpt, as Choice *C* indicates, and Mr. Button does put on clothes, as Choice *D* indicates. However, Mr. Button is not going to the doctor's office nor is he about to go shopping for new clothes.

2. A: The tone of the above passage is nervous and excited. We are told in the fourth paragraph that Mr. Button "arose nervously." We also see him running without caution to the doctor to find out about his wife and baby—this indicates his excitement. We also see him stuttering in a nervous yet excited fashion as he asks the doctor if it's a boy or girl. Though the doctor may seem a bit abrupt at the end, indicating a bit of anger or shame, neither of these choices is the overwhelming tone of the entire passage.

3. C: Dedicated. Mr. Button is dedicated to the task before him. Choice *A*, numbed, Choice *B*, chained, and Choice *D*, moved, all could grammatically fit in the sentence. However, they are not synonyms with *consecrated* like Choice *C* is.

4. D: Giving readers a visual picture of what the doctor is doing. The author describes a visual image— the doctor rubbing his hands together—first and foremost. The author may be trying to make a comment about the profession; however, the author does not "explain the detail of the doctor's profession" as Choice *B* suggests.

5. D: To introduce the setting of the story and its characters. We know we are being introduced to the setting because we are given the year in the very first paragraph along with the season: "one day in the summer of 1860." This is a classic structure of an introduction of the setting. We are also getting a long explanation of Mr. Button, what his work is, who is related to him, and what his life is like in the third paragraph.

6. B: "Talk sense!" is an example of an imperative sentence. An imperative sentence gives a command. The doctor is commanding Mr. Button to talk sense. Choice *A* is an example of an exclamatory sentence, which expresses excitement. Choice *C* is an example of an interrogative sentence—these types of sentences ask questions. Choice *D* is an example of a declarative sentence. This means that the character is simply making a statement.

7. B: The word *anachronism* most nearly means misplacement. Choice *A*, comparison, is an analogy or similarity to something. Choice *C*, *aberration*, means abnormality. Choice *D*, *amelioration*, means improvement.

8. C: This passage can best be described as a narrative, which is a type of passage that tells a story. Choice *A*, expository, is a text organized logically to investigate a problem. Choice *B*, descriptive, is a text that mostly goes about describing something or someone in detail. Choice *D*, persuasive, is a text that is organized as an argument and meant to persuade the audience to do something.

9. A: To explain the setting of the narrative and give information about the story. The setting of a narrative is the time and place. We see from the first paragraph that the year is 1860. We also can discern that it is summer, and Mr. and Mrs. Button are about to have a baby. This tells us both the setting and information about the story.

10. D: Something is unusual about the birth of the baby. The word "curious" is thrown in at the end twice, which tells us the doctor is suspicious about something having to do with the birth of the baby, since that is the most recent event to happen. Mr. Button is acting like a father who is expecting a baby, and the doctor seems confused about something.

11. C: This is a tricky question, but it can be solved through careful context analysis and vocabulary knowledge. One can infer that the use of "expedient," while not necessarily very positive, isn't inherently bad in this context either. Note how in the next line, he says, "but most governments are usually, and all governments are sometimes, inexpedient." This use of "inexpedient" indicates that a government becomes a hindrance rather than a solution; it slows progress rather than helps facilitate progress. Thus, Choice *A* and Choice *D* can be ruled out because these are more of the result of government, not the intention or initial design. Choice *B* makes no logical sense. Therefore, Choice *C* is the best description of *expedient.* Essentially, Thoreau is saying that government is constructed as a way of developing order and people's rights, but the rigidness of government soon inhibits justice and human rights.

12. B: While Choice *D* is the only answer that mentions the Mexican War directly, Thoreau clearly thinks the war is unnecessary because the people generally didn't consent to the war. Choices *A*, *B*, and *C* are all correct to a degree, but the answer asks for the best description. Therefore, Choice *B* is the most accurate representation of Thoreau's views. Essentially, Thoreau brings to light the fact that the few people in power can twist government and policy for their own needs.

13. D: Choices *A* and *B* are completely incorrect. Thoreau is not defending government in any way. His views are set against government. As mentioned in the text, he appreciates little government but favors having no government structure at all. The text is reflective by nature but not reflective on the stages of government abuses as Choice *C* suggests. Choice *D* is the more appropriate answer because of the presence of evidence in the text. Thoreau cites current events and uses them to illustrate the point he's trying to make.

14. C: One of Thoreau's biggest criticisms of government is its capacity to impose on the people's freedoms and liberties, enacting rules that the people don't want and removing power from the individual. None of the scenarios directly impose specific regulations or restrictions on the people, except Prohibition. Prohibition removed the choice to consume alcohol in favor of abstinence, which was favored by the religious conservatives of the time. Thus, Thoreau would point out that this is a clear violation of free choice and an example of government meddling.

15. A: Choice *B* is totally irrelevant. Choice *C* is also incorrect; Thoreau never personifies government. Also, this doesn't coincide with his wooden gun analogy. Choice *D* is compelling because of its language but doesn't define the statement. Choice *A* is the most accurate summary of the main point of Thoreau's statement.

16. B: Thoreau specifically cites that legislators "are continually putting in their way." This reflects his suspicion and concern of government intervention. Recall that Thoreau continually mentions that government, while meant as a way to establish freedom, is easily used to suppress freedom, piling on regulations and rules that inhibit progress. Choice *B* is the answer that most directly states how Thoreau sees government getting in the way of freedom.

17. D: This passage is an expository essay, which means that an idea is investigated and then expanded upon. Thoreau is investigating the idea of government here and how the U.S. government works in relation to the people.

18. C: The word *liable* most nearly means susceptible. The text says, "The government itself, which is only the mode which the people have chosen to execute their will, is equally liable to be abused and perverted before the people can act through it." Thoreau is saying here that the government is vulnerable enough to be abused. Choice *A*, *paramount*, means having importance. Choice *B*, *inconceivable*, means unbelievable. Choice *D*, *detrimental*, means damaging.

19. B: Thoreau is talking about the American government. We see this information in the beginning of the second paragraph. The passage mentions the Mexican War, but the passage itself does not relay the vulnerabilities of the Mexican government. The other two countries are not mentioned in the passage.

20. B: Posterity means all future generations of people. The sentence would say, "The American government—what is it but a tradition, though a recent one, endeavoring to transmit itself unimpaired to all future generations of people . . ." Choice *A* would be the definition of *royalty*. Choice *C* would be the definition of an *educator*. Choice *D* would be the definition of a *philosopher*.

21. A: Choice *D* can be eliminated because the Salem witch trials aren't mentioned. While sympathetic to the plight of the accused, the author doesn't demand or urge the reader to demand reparations to the descendants; therefore, Choice *B* can also be ruled out. It's clear that the author's main goal is to educate the reader and shed light on the facts and hidden details behind the case. However, his focus isn't on the occult, but the specific Lancashire case itself. He goes into detail about suspects' histories and ties to Catholicism, revealing how the fears of the English people at the time sealed the fate of the accused witches. Choice *A* is correct.

22. B: It's important to note that these terms may not be an exact analog for *enduring*. However, through knowledge of the definition of *enduring*, as well as the context in which it's used, an appropriate synonym can be found. Plugging "circumstantial" into the passage in place of "enduring" doesn't make sense. Nor does "un-original," this particular case of witchcraft, stand out in history. "Wicked" is very descriptive, but this is an attribute applied to people, not events; therefore, this is an inappropriate choice as well. *Enduring* literally means long lasting, referring to the continued interest in this particular case of witchcraft. Therefore, it's a popular topic of 1600s witch trials, making "popular," Choice *B*, the best choice.

23. D: Choices *A* and *B* are irrelevant and incorrect. The use of quotes lends credibility to the author. However, the presence of quotes alone doesn't necessarily mean that the author has a qualified perspective. What establishes the writer as a reliable voice is that the author's previous writing on the subject has been published before. This qualification greatly establishes the author's credentials as a historical writer, making Choice *D* the correct answer.

24. B: Choice *B* is the best answer because it ultimately encompasses the potentiality of Choices *C* and *D*. Choice *A* is incorrect because it takes the statement literally. For Choice *C*, it's possible that evidence was tampered with or even falsified, but this statement doesn't refer to this. While the author alludes that there may have been evidence tampering and potentially corruption (Choice *D*), what the writer is directly saying is that the documentation of the court indicates an elaborate trial.

25. C: Several of these answers could have contributed to the fear and political motivations around the Lancashire witch trials. What this answer's looking for is very specific: political motivations and issues that played a major role in the case. Choice *C* clearly outlines the public fears of the time. It also describes how the government can use this fear to weed out and eliminate traces of Catholicism (and witchcraft too). Catholicism and witchcraft were seen as dangerous and undermining to English Protestantism and governance. Choice *D* can be eliminated; while this information may have some truth

and is certainly consistent with the general fear of witchcraft, the details about Lancashire's ancient history aren't mentioned in the text. Choice *A* is true but not necessarily political in nature. Choice *B* is very promising, though not outright mentioned.

26. D: The best evidence comes from Alizon herself. The text mentions that she confessed to bewitching John Law, thinking that she did him harm. From here she names her grandmother, who she believes corrupted her. Choice *B* can be ruled out; spectral evidence isn't mentioned. The case draws on knowledge of superstition of witchcraft, but this in itself can't be considered evidence, so Choice *A* is incorrect. Choice *C* isn't evidence in a modern sense; rumors have no weight in court and therefore are not evidence. While this is used as evidence to some degree, this still isn't the *best* evidence against Alizon and the witches.

27. B: This type of passage would be considered expository, which is an informative passage. Choice *A*, persuasive, means to take a side of an argument, and this essay is merely divulging information. Choice *C*, narrative, means to tell a story. Although a story is being told indirectly, the essay doesn't follow a traditional narrative. Choice *D*, descriptive, means a detailed description of a person or place.

28. B: According to the passage, 20 people were arrested as witches in the Lancashire trials. The essay tells us that "ten were hanged, one died in goal (jail), one was sentenced to death in the pillory, and eight were acquitted."

29. D: The word *commemorative* means in honor of something. The context clue here includes the "works of fiction" by the authors Blake Morrison, Ann Duffy, and Jeanette Winterson, no doubt to celebrate the preserved history of the famous trial.

30. C: Malkin tower is the house of Alizon's grandmother. It is also a place where a meeting of witches was said to be held in the passage. The passage says, "The net was widened still further at the end of April when Alizon's younger brother James and younger sister Jennet, only nine years old, came up between them with a story about a "great meeting of witches" at their grandmother's house, known as Malkin Tower."

31. A: It introduces certain insects that transition from water to air. Choice *B* is incorrect because although the passage talks about gills, it is not the central idea of the passage. Choices *C* and *D* are incorrect because the passage does not "define" or "invite," but only serves as an introduction to stoneflies, dragonflies, and mayflies and their transition from water to air.

32. C: The act of shedding part or all of the outer shell. Choices *A*, *B*, and *D* are incorrect. The word in the passage is mentioned here: "But it is advisable in connection with our present subject to dwell especially on some insects that remain continually under water till they are ready to undergo their final moult and attain the winged state, which they pass entirely in the air."

33. B: The first paragraph serves as a contrast to the second. Notice how the first paragraph goes into detail describing how insects are able to breathe air. The second paragraph acts as a contrast to the first by stating "[i]t is of great interest to find that, nevertheless, a number of insects spend much of their time under water." Watch for transition words such as "nevertheless" to help find what type of passage you're dealing with.

34: C: The stage of preparation in between molting is acted out in the water, while the last stage is in the air. Choices *A*, *B*, and *D* are all incorrect. *Instars* is the phase between two periods of molting, and the text explains when these transitions occur.

35. C: The author's tone is informative and exhibits interest in the subject of the study. Overall, the author presents us with information on the subject. One moment where personal interest is depicted is when the author states, "It is of great interest to find that, nevertheless, a number of insects spend much of their time under water."

36. C: Their larva can breathe the air dissolved in water through gills of some kind. This is stated in the last paragraph. Choice *A* is incorrect because the text mentions this in a general way at the beginning of the passage concerning "insects as a whole." Choice *B* is incorrect because this is stated of beetles and water-bugs, and not the insects in question. Choice *D* is incorrect because this is the opposite of what the text says of instars.

37. B: According to the passage, boatmen and scorpions have some way of protecting their spiracles when submerged. We see this in the second paragraph, which says "(boatmen and scorpions) which have some way of protecting their spiracles when submerged."

38. A: The best answer Choice is *A*: the author believes that the stonefly, dragonfly, and mayfly larvae are better prepared to live beneath the water because they have gills that allow them to do so. We see this when the author says "But the larva of a stone-fly, a dragon-fly, or a may-fly is adapted more completely than these for aquatic life; it can, by means of gills of some kind, breathe the air dissolved in water."

39. C: Because a vast majority of insects have wings and also have the ability to breathe underwater. The entire first paragraph talks of how insects have wings, and how insects also have "a system of branching air-tubes" that carries oxygen to the insect's tissues.

40. B: The word *preeminently* most nearly means *above all* or *in particular*. The author is saying that above all, insects are creatures of both land and water.

Listening

The Listening section test of the TOEFL iBT® lasts between 60 and 90 minutes and consists of 34–51 questions. These ranges exist because Educational Testing Service (ETS) sometimes includes additional questions in the Listening section that enable test developers to assess the viability of potential future scored questions or to compare outcomes of various administrations of the TOEFL across the country, as benchmark questions. While test takers are not alerted to which test questions fall under either of these conditions, the experimental questions are unscored and as such, they do not affect one's results either way.

As mentioned, there are 34–51 questions on the Listening section of the TOEFL iBT®, which follow each listening clip. There are six questions per lecture or academic discussion and five questions following each conversation. Depending on the inclusion of the unscored experimental section, the section includes 4–6 lectures and academic discussions, each of which is 3–5 minutes in duration, and 2–3 more casual conversations that each last approximately three minutes.

When you get to the listening practice questions, you can find all of our recordings here:

testprepbooks.com/toefl

All of the questions are multiple choice; the majority offer four answer choices of which test takers must select the single best choice, although some multiple-choice questions may require selecting two or more correct answers. Some questions go beyond regurgitating the information that was presented in the recording and ask test takers to demonstrate deeper listening comprehension by making inferences or describing emotions or other implicit details. Some questions may involve categorizing items using charts or tables or require test takers to order steps or events in a sequence.

It should be noted that not all of the speakers in the audio recordings in the Listening section may speak with native North American English accents. Test takers may encounter English speakers with native accents from the United Kingdom, New Zealand, and Australia.

ETS test administrators model the TOEFL iBT® Listening section exercises after typical classroom lectures, discussions, or common administrative tasks that test takers will encounter in real-world settings long after passing the TOEFL iBT®. Lecture topics pull from a variety of academic disciplines in the arts and sciences, such as history, psychology, earth science, economics, and sociology. Some lecture exercises will be delivered by a single speaker, who is an instructor, or they may feature several speakers in a classroom discussion format, often between the instructor and a handful of students. For example, the instructor may give a short lecture about architecture and then pause to call on a couple of students to answer questions pertaining to the material just presented, or a student may ask the instructor a clarifying question. After the instructor answers the student's question, he or she may continue with the lecture or segue into an organic conversation that deviates from the original lecture topic but more fully answers the student's question.

The conversations revolve around typical interactions encountered around a university setting between a variety of individuals such as coaches, students, secretaries, administrators, and roommates. Topics may include conversations about registering for classes, purchasing textbooks, asking for directions or locating buildings around campus, meeting a roommate, receiving feedback on an assignment, and asking for academic support, among many others. The speech in the conversations is meant to sound natural and duplicate that which normally occurs between people, including imperfections and pauses. Characters may stumble over their words or even use the wrong word sometimes; test takers may be asked to point out these errors in the questions that follow the recording.

Test takers are allowed to listen to each exercise only one time, although they are encouraged to take notes while they listen, which they can refer to while answering the questions that follow the clip. If headsets are provided, they will have adjustable volume that test takers can experiment with prior to listening to the scored exercises. Each listening exercise begins with a picture of some sort to provide context for the conversation or lecture, and longer recordings will have additional pictures or diagrams scattered throughout the 3–5-minute clip.

ETS presents test takers with three categories of questions on the Listening section and both the lectures and conversations feature questions in each of these categories.

- **Basic Conversation Questions** are one of three types: **Gist-content questions** address the overall general content of the lecture, discussion, or conversation. Instead of addressing the broad content of the lectures or conversations, **gist-purpose questions** require test takers to identify the primary reasons for the given lectures or discussion. Lastly, **detail questions** ask test takers about specific facts provided in the lectures or regarding specific details from the conversations.

- **Pragmatic Understanding Questions** can be one of two types. In the first type, test takers must demonstrate their understanding of the speaker's purpose for delivering certain statements, or the function of what was said. In the second type, test takers must identify the speaker's emotions or preferences, often using nuances in tone of voice, inflection, and intonation to detect attitudes such as sarcasm, frustration, disappointment, or irony.

- **Connecting and Synthesizing Information Questions** can be one of three types. The **understanding organization** questions require test takers to select answer choices that correctly reflect the structure of the listening exercise or the function of specific statements delivered in the lecture or conversation. The **connecting content** questions are the only type of question that is solely found in the lecture-based exercises. It involves demonstrating relationships between explicit and implicit ideas presented in the lecture and often includes charts or tables that test takers must interpret to successfully answer the question. Finally, the **making inferences** questions involve using statements in the conversations or lectures to draw conclusions or surmise information that may not be explicitly discussed in the listening exercise.

Test takers often find the Listening section daunting, particularly because exercises can only be played once. However, the following are a couple of helpful strategies that successful test takers employ to achieve high scores in this section:

- **Use the pictures**: The initial picture helps set the stage and helps provide the context for conversation or lecture that test takers are about to hear. This picture is crucial in helping the listener imagine what is happening and visualize the speakers before the dialogue even begins. The additional pictures and visual aids that are presented during the course of the audio recordings appear in coordination with the statements or events in the lectures and conversations as they unfurl. Again, these are powerful aids to add context clues about the

setting, speakers, and content, which, when taken with the audio information, helps provide test takers with a more complete and comprehensive understanding of the exercise.

- **Take notes**: Test takers can, and should, take notes while they listen to the recording that they can refer to while answering questions. While it is most important to devote attention towards critical listening, jotting down a few key points or details that seem important can help jog one's memory after the recording is over when the questions are presented. Some questions ask very specific information, and this is where careful listening with an ear towards details and a couple of key notes can be quite helpful. For example, from a conversation between two roommates buying course textbooks at the campus store, test takers may be asked to recall the specific subjects for which one speaker was buying books.

- **Practice**: The importance of practice cannot be overstated. Successful test takers listen to spoken English every chance they get and try to understand the main points, supporting details, and the emotions and attitudes of the speakers. There are a variety of mediums that present listening opportunities from television programs and movies to podcasts and audiobooks. In-person opportunities include class lectures, conversations with peers and friends, interactions with customer service agents, among others. While formal questions aren't presented after most listening opportunities, candidates can assess their understanding by listening to recordings several times or asking speakers of in-person conversations clarifying questions to verify understanding.

- **Listen for verbal cues**: Listeners can gather clues by appreciating the verbal cues from the recordings. Word emphasis, tone of voice, pauses interjected for effect, and changes in voice inflection can communicate implicit information such as the speaker's emotion (surprise, worry, frustration, etc.) or emphasize that something important is about to happen. Again, understanding these nuances in spoken language will help test takers more fully grasp the meaning of the conversation or lecture in the recordings.

Practice Questions

Directions: The Listening section measures your ability to understand conversations and lectures in English. In this test, you will listen to several pieces of content and answer questions after each one. The questions typically ask about the main idea and supporting details. Some questions ask about a speaker's purpose or attitude. Answer the questions based on what is stated or implied by the speakers.

Listen to all of these passages here:

> **testprepbooks.com/toefl**

Note that on the actual test, you can take notes while you listen and use your notes to help you answer the questions. Your notes will not be scored.

For your convenience, the transcripts of all of the audio passages are provided after the answer explanations. However, on the actual test, no such transcripts will be provided.

Passage #1: Conversation

Listen to the audio here: testprepbooks.com/toefl

1. What was Greg looking for help with?
    a. Biology class material
    b. Studying economics
    c. Getting off campus to run errands
    d. Finding the administration building

2. How does a student replace their campus ID according to Deborah? Mark all that apply.
    a. Go to the library by the encyclopedias
    b. Go to the administration building
    c. Fill out a form and show a picture ID
    d. Pay a replacement fee

3. Where did Greg lose his ID?
    a. At the movies
    b. In biology class
    c. Grocery shopping
    d. At the basketball game

4. Where is the library?
    a. Next to the dining hall on the main quad
    b. Across from the dining hall on the main quad
    c. Away from the main quad near the administration building
    d. Next to the dorms on the main quad

5. Read the following statement from the conversation and then answer the question:
Male student: I haven't really gotten into a study rhythm yet this semester. That may be part of my problem. I guess I study in my room, when my roommate and I aren't playing video games, that is.

What does the male student mean when he says he has not really gotten into "a study rhythm yet"?

    a. He has not yet studied with music
    b. He needs to study with video games
    c. He has not yet established a study routine or habit
    d. He only studies in the library after class

6. Why does the female student say: "Well, I've got to run to Economics class now"?
    a. She is preparing to end the conversation
    b. She enjoys running for the school's track team
    c. She is trying to change the topic of conversation
    d. She wants a ride to class because she has to get there quickly

Passage #2: Lecture

Listen to the audio here: testprepbooks.com/toefl

7. What is the main topic of the lecture?
    a. The range of learning disabilities that future teachers should be aware of
    b. The ways in which Executive Functioning Disorder impacts students
    c. The cures for Executive Functioning Disorder
    d. How to teach students who are interested in psychology

8. What is the role of the executive function of the brain?
    a. To make business decisions for the brain and body
    b. To plan, organize, and manage tasks, processes, and deadlines
    c. To prevent learning disabilities
    d. To help take notes, listen to lectures, and perform well on exams

9. Why does the professor explain in detail how teachers can modify their instruction to help students with Executive Functioning Disorder?
    a. Because many of the students listening to the lecture want to become teachers
    b. Because many of the students listening to the lecture have Executive Functioning Disorder
    c. Because Executive Functioning Disorder only affects students in school
    d. Because the students listening to the lecture are teachers

10. What does the professor mean by: While executive functioning issues alone can have a significant impact on an individual, I want you to think about how it often um...appears concurrently with other learning disorders like ADHD or dyslexia.
    a. Executive Function Disorder is worse than ADHD or dyslexia
    b. Executive Functioning Disorder is discussed in the same lecture as ADHD and dyslexia
    c. People with Executive Functioning Disorder visually look a certain way
    d. People with Executive Function Disorders often have other learning disabilities too

11. Why does the professor add the clause "Like in our class" to the beginning of the sentence: "Like in our class, teachers should review prior material briefly before building upon it in the new lesson"?
  a. To help students connect the lesson with their own experience
  b. To remind students of their learning disabilities
  c. To show students that he is a good professor
  d. To persuade students to become teachers

12. Read the following sentences from the lecture and then answer the question:
"They also may find analyzing ideas and identifying when and how to seek help to be a challenge. Let's see...heeding attention to and remembering details is also encumbered."

Encumbered most nearly means which of the following?

  a. Hindered
  b. Enticing
  c. Important
  d. Recognized

13. Based on the information in the lecture, which of the following would someone with Executive Functioning Disorder likely struggle with?
  a. Reading a fantasy novel
  b. Playing sports on a team
  c. Remembering what to buy in the grocery store without a list
  d. Painting or drawing realistic landscapes

Passage #3: Lecture

Listen to the audio here: testprepbooks.com/toefl

Narrator: Listen to part of a lecture from astronomy class and then answer the questions.

Female Professor: We are continuing our discussion today of the history of astronomers from ancient times working up to the present day. So, remember, we are talking about the key contributors that have helped build our understanding of astronomy today. Let's pick up now with Nicolaus Copernicus. Copernicus, in many ways, can be thought of as the first in the modern astronomy scientists because he overturned the geocentric model of the solar system that had stood for over two thousand years, and instead, correctly (but shockingly at the time) suggested that the sun was the center of the solar system and the planets revolved around the sun. This was basically the birth of our present understanding of the solar system – the Heliocentric model. Before we go on, I want to remind you about the geocentric model we talked about last class. Remember, the ancient Greeks believed in a geocentric model of the universe, such that the planets and stars rotated around the central, stationary Earth. But Copernicus recognized that the uh...that the moon rotated around the Earth and that the Earth is just one of several planets revolving around the Sun. He also noted that the Sun is a star, the closest star, and other stars are much further away, that Earth rotates around its axis every day in addition to its yearly revolution, and that closer planets have shorter "years." Pretty important discoveries, huh?

Then we have Tycho Brahe. Now, Brahe was instrumental in determining the positions of fixed stars, unaided by telescopes, which were not yet invented. He made astronomical tools to help

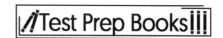

with mapping and understanding the "heavens" and the Solar System. He thought the Earth was not moving and that the Sun and Moon revolved around the stationary planet, so we know now that this part was off-base, but he's still a key player in our evolution.

Johannes Kepler was interested in math and astronomy and felt that geometric figures influenced the universe. He built upon Copernicus' heliocentric model and you've probably heard of his three Laws of Planetary Motion. The first law states that planetary orbits are elliptical, not circular, and the Sun is at one of the foci and not the center. The second law says that the planetary speed is faster near the sun and slower when it is more distant. The third law is somewhat similar. This one states that um...that the larger the orbit of a planet, the slower its average velocity.

Next, we have Galileo Galilei. That's a fun name to say. Well, Galileo made many advancements to our thinking and to our ability to make further discoveries, like he invented the telescope. He used it to observe sunspots and discovered that the lunar surface, like Earth, had mountains and valleys. Let's see...he also noted that the Milky Way galaxy had separate stars, he discovered moons around Jupiter, and designed instruments such as a compass and this neat little calculating device. These discoveries helped prove the universe was dynamic and changing. Perhaps most importantly, he lay the foundations for scientific thought and process, the importance of logic and reason, and how to do experiments.

Lastly, Sir Isaac Newton. Remember, Newton was the one that proposed the three laws of motion that I'm sure you've heard in physics class: an object in motion stays in motion and an object at rest stays at rest unless acted on by an external force, force equals mass times acceleration, and every action has an equal and opposite reaction. He also proposed the Universal Law of Gravitation, which states that gravity is a force and that every object in the Universe is attracted to every other object. The magnitude of this force is directly proportional to the product of the masses of the objects and inversely proportional to the square of the distances between them.

14. What was the main topic addressed in the lecture?
    a. The contributions of various historical astronomers to our understanding of modern astronomy
    b. The importance of the telescope in our understanding of the Universe
    c. The history of how the Universe and Solar System formed
    d. The geocentric model of the Solar System

15. According to the professor, what was Copernicus' main contribution to our understanding?
    a. He proposed the geocentric model of the Solar System
    b. He invented the telescope, which we have used to make more discoveries
    c. He proposed the three laws of motion
    d. He developed the idea that Earth, and the other planets, rotate around the Sun

16. How was the information in the lecture organized?
    a. In order of importance of each scientist's discoveries
    b. In chronological order of the scientists' work
    c. In the order presented in the course textbook
    d. In the order of how many discoveries each scientist made

17. What does the professor imply about the scientists discussed in the lecture?
   a. That only their accurate discoveries or proposals were important to our understanding
   b. That they made a lot of mistakes in their discoveries
   c. That they did not know very much about the Universe
   d. That their contributions, even when inaccurate. helped shape our current understanding

18. Which of the following are attributed to Galileo? Pick two answers.
   a. He proposed the three laws of motion
   b. He said the Sun was a star
   c. He invented the telescope
   d. He lay the foundation for scientific thought and experimentation

19. Listen again to the sentences about Brahe and then answer the question.
(heard again) He thought the Earth was not moving and that the Sun and Moon revolved around the stationary planet, so we know now that this part was off-base but he's still a key player in our evolution.

What does the professor imply about Brahe in this sentence?

   a. That his ideas were wrong and not important in the discussion of astronomy
   b. That other scientists and other humans continued to evolve from his DNA
   c. That he made a bunch of discoveries we have verified as correct
   d. That he is important in any discussion of the history of astronomy, even if some of his ideas were incorrect

Passage #4: Lecture and Discussion

Listen to the audio here: testprepbooks.com/toefl

Narrator: Listen to the following portion of a lecture and discussion from a geology class.

Male Professor: So now I want to turn our discussion to your homework assignment, Anne Sasso's article in *Discover* magazine called "The Geology of...Rubies." This article discussed how rubies are formed, why they have been so enamored throughout history, and what causes their brilliant red color, which, as I hope you read, is due to the ultraviolet light from the Sun causing the chromium in rubies to glow. Geologists are still searching for reasons as to how the existence of rubies came to be. Do you remember how Penn State University Geosciences professor Peter Heaney referred to rubies as a "minor geological miracle"? Can anyone tell me why Dr. Heaney says this?

Male student: Basically, he's saying um...that the formation of rubies is essentially a perfect storm and a rare occurrence. It's like a miracle that they ever form.

Male professor: Exactly, Xavier. Rubies are a specific type of the rare mineral corundum, which is composed of densely packed aluminum and oxygen atoms. These atoms are normally colorless, but when other atoms, like in this case chromium, are substituted for a some of the uh...aluminum ones, the deep red color of rubies is produced. Other substitutions cause the bright colors of other gemstones such as sapphire from the substitution of um, uh...from titanium and iron. Corundum is rare, the elemental substitutions are rare, chromium itself is rare, and even *more* rare is the fact that this cannot occur in the presence of silica or large amounts of iron, and silica is one of the most abundant elements in the crust and iron is

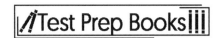

common too but must be in very low concentrations to form rubies. This can kind of be visualized as hmmm...like a Venn diagram of increasingly more rare occurrences and just a tiny overlapped center where the formation of this geone is actually possible.

Does anyone remember from the article how rubies form?

Female student: Was that the part about how they are used for jewelry and even people centuries ago marveled at their beauty?

Professor: Well that's more about their importance or our interest in them. I'm looking for how they are created geologically.

Female student: Oh! Oops. Yeah, they form through plate tectonics, particularly at the boundary by the um, um...Himalayas, where deposits of the sedimentary rock limestone get pushed under the other plate and metamorphosed into the marble.

Professor: Exactly Claudia! Molten granite in magma percolates in and infiltrates the forming marble. This limestone and granite interaction contains the chemical elements we now know are present in rubies. Importantly, this process removes the silica but left the aluminum. Geologist can even date the formation of these gemstones with the tectonic movements. Even more recently, teams of scientists have found that salt played an integral role in the formation of the rubies because it allowed the aluminum atoms to be fluid enough to get displaced occasionally by chromium.

Does anyone have any questions?... Yes, Xavier.

Male student: Have geologists done experiments to try to recreate all these conditions at once to make all different kinds of gemstones in the lab?

Professor: Well, kind of. Remember...scientists typically only address one question at a time so that they can use the scientific method. This method establishes a rigorous process of investigation so that it can be uh...replicated by other scientists to verify results. By focusing on just one hypothesis, scientists should only manipulate a single variable at a time, called the independent variable, and then examine its results on the dependent variable. What would happen if scientists didn't carefully isolate variables?

Female student: Well, if scientists were to manipulate multiple variables, it would be impossible to know which change resulted in the observed effects.

Professor: You got it! If scientists were to work to investigate multiple questions or change more than one variable when conducting an experiment, the research would be scattered, unfocused, and unable to prove anything.

20. What is the main topic of the lecture?
   a. The scientific method and how to conduct experiments
   b. How gemstones are used for jewelry
   c. Why rubies are rare and how they form
   d. How to read articles in *Discover* magazine

21. Why did Penn State University Geosciences professor Peter Heaney refer to rubies as a "minor geological miracle"?
    a. Because conditions must be perfect for them to form and this is rare
    b. Because they are important gemstones that contribute to our economy
    c. Because they can be discovered through scientific experiments
    d. Because they are red

22. According to the professor, how do gemstones get their colors?
    a. By the different temperature under which they form
    b. By forming in volcanoes or in the Himalayas, areas that have lots of color
    c. By various elemental substitutions to the normal arrangement of aluminum and oxygen atoms.
    d. By jewelers looking to design beautiful, ornate designs that consumers will buy

23. Based on what the professor says about conducting scientific experiments, which of the following experiments would he likely recommend for making the best chocolate chip cookies?
    a. An experiment that manipulates baking conditions by cooking batches at different temperatures and for different lengths of time
    b. An experiment that adds different amounts of sugar and bakes them for different lengths of time
    c. An experiment that adds different proportions of whole wheat and white flower, different amounts of sugar, and bakes them for different lengths of time
    d. An experiment that uses the same exact recipe but bakes them for different lengths of time

24. According to the lecture, where are rubies formed?
    a. At the boundaries of different plates, where sedimentary rock gets pushed under the other plate and gets metamorphosed
    b. In magma percolating under a volcano
    c. Abundantly in the Himalayas
    d. Where aluminum and oxygen come together in a Venn diagram

25. According to the discussion, which of the following are true about rubies? Select two correct answers.
    a. They are gemstones
    b. They readily form
    c. They are a variety of corundum
    d. We have no idea how old they are

Passage #5: Conversation

Listen to the audio here: testprepbooks.com/toefl

Narrator: Listen to the following conversation between a student and the school's financial aid officer.

Female student: Hi. Is this the right place to ask about a problem with my bill?

Male officer: Yes. This is the financial aid office so I can assist you with any tuition and billing questions.

Female student: Great. So, I received my bill for the semester and it says I owe $18000. I thought I had a scholarship so there's no way I can pay this bill, plus now there's a hold on my account so I can't seem to register for classes and I'm worried they are going to fill up.

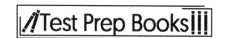

Male officer: Ok let's see. Do you have a copy of your bill with you?

Female student: No. I left it in my dorm by accident.

Male officer: No problem. Can I see your student ID? I can pull it up in our system.

Female student: Yes. Here it is. Don't mind the picture. I didn't know I was going to be photographed that day!

Male officer: Oh, don't be silly...you look nice! Ok. Let me just take a look here at your bill and see what's going on. Hmm...Yes, I see the tuition billed to your account is $8500. Your meal plan and housing in the dorms is $7,000 this semester and there is a technology fee and other posted fees including your parking permit totaling $2500. The total amount posted to your account is $18000.

Female student: What about my scholarship?

Male officer: Well, it looks like you have a scholarship that is pending in your account for the amount of tuition, the $8500. It has not been applied because we are waiting on your financial aid application. Did you fill out the FAFSA? We need a current copy of that on file.

Female student: No. I didn't know I needed to do that.

Male officer: You'll definitely want to get that in as soon as possible. That way we can process your scholarship and also if you qualify for additional financial aid, we can set up a package for you. Some students get additional scholarships based on financial need, or there are loans, and work-study opportunities.

Female student: Oh, that sounds helpful. What is work-study?

Male officer: Work study refers to campus-based jobs where the compensation for you comes directly off of your bill. There are a variety of available positions for students around campus like in the library, at the sports center, or even in one of the administrative offices.

Female student: Ok cool. Back home I worked as a computer programmer at my mom's software company.

Male officer: Well we have lots of office positions too. So, what you need to do first is register to fill out FASFA on the website. You'll need to put in last year's tax information, so make sure you have that as well. Then, they will evaluate your financial aid package to determine what your needs are. If you want to do a work-study you can apply for a campus job. Lastly, make sure you pay the remaining balance on your account so that you can register for classes.

Female student: Ok thanks. I better get going on this!

26. What is the main problem the student is having?
    a. She does not know which classes to register for
    b. She needs to get a job on campus
    c. Her bill is higher than she predicted
    d. She is looking for financial aid forms

27. Which of the following are ways that students can receive financial assistance with their school bills?
    a. Scholarships
    b. Loans
    c. Work-study
    d. Tuition

28. When would be the best time for students to speak to a financial aid officer?
    a. At 12:30pm on a Tuesday
    b. Saturday mornings
    c. At 4:15pm on Monday
    d. At 2:00pm on Wednesday

29. Which of the following were components of the student's bill? Select all that apply.
    a. Tuition
    b. Technology fee
    c. Meal plan and housing
    d. Activities fee

30. The financial aid officer explains to the student what she needs to do to fill out her FASFA, apply for a work-study, and fix the hold on her account. In what order does he list the steps?

A. Register for classes		1	
B. Apply for a campus job		2	
C. Wait for evaluation of financial aid package		3	
D. Pay balance on the account		4	
E. Register to fill out the FAFSA		5	
F. Input prior year's tax information		6	
G. Ask for tuition reduction			

31. Based on the conversation, which job is the student most likely to apply for?
    a. A job at the financial aid office
    b. A job at the computer lab
    c. A job at the sports center
    d. A job at the library

Passage #6: Lecture Discussion

Listen to the audio here: testprepbooks.com/toefl

32. What was the main topic of the discussion between the professor and her students?
    a. The importance of literature
    b. The themes in *Gulliver's Travels*
    c. The literal meaning in Swift's book
    d. The reasons that Gulliver travels

33. What does the professor mean when she says, "I want to dig deeper into this thought…"
    a. She needs to uncover a time capsule that she has buried
    b. She needs to unearth her copy of the book on her desk
    c. She wants to bury the conversation
    d. She wants to explore this topic more

34. Why might the professor say, "Name-dropping is our modern equivalent to Gulliver's boasting about his close relationships with Kings and Queens!"
    a. To help students remember the names of all of the characters in the book
    b. To help students understand things in the book by relating it to things they are familiar with
    c. To remind students that everyone forgets names, so not to worry
    d. To show empathy towards Gulliver

35. What does the professor argue is the value of reading *Gulliver's Travels*?
    a. For entertainment value
    b. To consider human nature and its imperfections
    c. To persuade readers to travel more, even though it is expensive
    d. To teach readers about all the kings and queens and faraway lands

36. According to the participants in the discussion, what would Swift's reaction be to humans being called "social animals"?
    a. Swift would disagree because he thinks humans are antisocial
    b. Swift would disagree because humans have high self-esteem
    c. Swift would agree because humans want to preserve their self-esteem
    d. Swift would agree because he thinks humans are very antisocial

Answer Explanations

1. A: At the beginning of the conversation, listeners should recall that the male student, Greg, was asking the female student, Deborah how she did on the biology exam. Deborah informs Greg that she did well, earning a 96, while Greg responds that he only got a 69. He says, "This stuff isn't making sense to me." *Stuff,* in this case, refers to the biology class material.

2. B, C, D: Deborah says that a student must go to the administration building with their student ID or another form of picture ID, pay a $15 replacement fee, and fill out a form. She mentions the encyclopedia section in the library in an earlier part of the conversation, referring to where she studies.

3. D: Greg says, "I lost my ID at the basketball game last weekend. Do you know where I can get a new one?"

4. B: Greg admits to Deborah that he's not honestly sure where the library is, and he asks her if it's over the dining hall on the main quad (the central square of a campus, which often has a grassy lawn and several main buildings surrounding it). Deborah's response confirms that Greg is in the ballpark, or close in his guess. She says, "Yes, it's over next to the administration building on the main quad, directly across from the dining hall." Test takers must carefully listen to select the correct answer. Choice *A* is incorrect because although the library is on the main quad, it is across from, rather than next to the dining hall, which is Choice *B*. Choice *C* is incorrect because although the library is next to the administration building, it is on the main quad. It is not near the dorms, so Choice *D* is incorrect.

5. C: When Greg says that he has not really gotten into "a study rhythm yet" he means that he has not yet established a study routine or habit.

6. A: Deborah says, "Well, I've got to run to Economics class now"" to signal that she is preparing to end the conversation. This is a common phrase used in casual conversation to convey that one person needs to leave and move on to the next thing and that he or she wants to end the conversation. She may not literally need to "run" to class, but she is wrapping up the conversation.

7. B: The main topic of the lecture is the ways in which Executive Functioning Disorder impacts students. Listeners hear about the symptoms of the disorder, how these symptoms play out in the classroom, and various techniques or accommodations that teachers may provide to assist a student with the disorder. Choice *A* is incorrect because while Executive Functioning Disorder is a learning disability and the professor mentions that the lecture is building upon previously discussed learning disabilities, the focus of the lecture is on the specific issue of Executive Functioning Disorder, not learning disabilities at large. Cures for the disorder are not mentioned, so Choice *C* is wrong, and while the students listening to the lecture are in a psychology class, the lecture is not about how to teach them, so Choice *D* is wrong.

8. B: The professor equates executive function of the brain to a CEO of a company because it is involved in the planning, organizing, and managing of tasks, processes, and deadlines. While it is helpful for the tasks in Choice *D* (taking notes, listening to lectures, and performing well on exams), these are examples of instances where it is used but does not refer to its general function overall.

9. A: The professor explains how teachers can modify their instruction to help students with Executive Functioning Disorder because many of the students listening to the lecture want to become teachers. This is evidenced by the fact that he says, "I know many of you have expressed an interest in teaching someday so uh…it's important to think about how this will affect students in your classrooms."

10. D: The professor ends the lecture clip by saying, "While executive functioning issues alone can have a significant impact on an individual, I want you to think about how it often um…appears concurrently with other learning disorders like ADHD or dyslexia." There are a few key words that indicate what this means. *While executive functioning issues alone can have a significant impact on an individual,* means that just having that single disorder can be challenging for a student. Then the next sentence uses the word *concurrently,* saying that it (executive functioning issues) often occur "concurrently with other learning disorders like ADHD or dyslexia." This means that they occur at the same time, so that someone can have both or multiple learning disabilities at once. This idea is further confirmed by his last statement: "This can make it, uh…especially challenging."

11. A: The professor says, "Like in our class, teachers should review prior material briefly before building upon it in the new lesson" to help students connect the lesson with their own experience in his classroom. Listeners get a glimpse into the fact that he has done this at the very beginning of the lecture. "Today, we are going to pick up where we left off last class talking about learning disabilities. Now, we will turn our attention to another common learning disability known as Executive Functioning Disorder." Teachers often try to connect concepts in the classroom to students' own experiences so that new material makes more sense and is relatable.

12. A: Read the following sentences from the lecture and then answer the question:

Encumbered most nearly means hindered or impeded. Even without knowing this vocabulary word, test takers can look for context clues to determine the meaning. The part of the passage in which that words appeared was mentioning difficulties or challenges faced by those with Executive Functioning Disorder. "They also may find analyzing ideas and identifying when and how to seek help to be a challenge. Let's see…heeding attention to and remembering details is also encumbered." It is clear that we are looking for a choice that signifies an issue, difficulty, or problem, making Choice *A* the only reasonable option.

13. C: Listeners learn that Executive Functioning Disorder causes difficulties with planning, organizing, and managing of tasks, processes, and deadlines. We also hear that they struggle to "memorize and especially retrieve things from their memory" which would make remembering what to buy in the grocery store without a list quite difficult.

14. A: This lecture is mainly focused on the contributions of various historical astronomers to our understanding of modern astronomy. While the telescope's importance is mentioned (Choice *B*), this is not the main topic of the lecture. Choice *C* is incorrect because the history of how the Universe and Solar System formed is not mentioned at all. The history of advancements in astronomy is, instead. Lastly, while the geocentric model of the Solar System is briefly discussed, it is not the primary topic in the lecture, as a much more significant portion of the talk is about notable advancements and discoveries, making Choice *D* incorrect.

15. D: The professor says, "Copernicus, in many ways, can be thought of as the first in the modern astronomy scientists because he overturned the geocentric model of the solar system that had stood for over two thousand years, and instead, correctly (but shockingly at the time) suggested that the sun was the center of the solar system and the planets revolved around the sun. This was basically the birth of our present understanding of the solar system – the Heliocentric model." This means that Copernicus developed the idea that Earth, and the other planets, rotate around the Sun, which overturned the geocentric model of the Solar System, making Choice *A* incorrect. Galileo invented the telescope so Choice *B* is wrong, and Newton proposed the three laws of motion, so Choice *C* is wrong.

16. B: The professor structures the lecture in chronological order of the scientists' work. Although dates are not provided, listeners can answer this correctly based on what the professor says at the beginning of the lecture: "We are *continuing* our discussion today of the history of astronomers *from ancient times working up to the present day*. So, remember, we are talking about the key contributors that have helped build our understanding of astronomy today."

17. D: The professor implies that the contributions of the discussed scientists, even when inaccurate, helped shape our current understanding of astronomy. Perhaps the best evidence for this argument comes from when she is talking about Brahe's importance, even though some of his ideas were incorrect. "He thought the Earth was not moving and that the Sun and Moon revolved around the stationary planet, so we know now that this part was off-base, *but he's still a key player in our evolution*."

18. C & D: Galileo invented the telescope and lay the foundation for scientific thought and experimentation. Newton proposed the three laws of motion, making Choice *A* incorrect and Copernicus said the Sun was a star, which makes Choice *B* wrong.

19. D: As mentioned, the selected statement implies that Brahe is important in any discussion of the history of astronomy, even if some of his ideas were incorrect. Choice *A* is incorrect because she said he *is* still important, Choice *C* is wrong because she is confirming that some of his ideas were incorrect, and Choice *B* is incorrect because "evolution" in this context isn't referring to human evolution or genetics, but the evolution or growth of our understanding of astronomy – how it is has changed over time.

20. C: The main topic of the lecture is why rubies are rare and how they form. Choice *A,* the scientific method and how to conduct experiments, is discussed, but is not the main focus of the talk. Choices *B* and *D* are barely touched upon, and therefore, are also incorrect.

21. A: Penn State University Geosciences professor Peter Heaney referred to rubies as a "minor geological miracle" because the conditions must be perfect for them to form and this is rare. This is, essentially, what the lecture discussion is all about. As the male student, Xavier, says, "Basically, he's saying um...that the formation of rubies is essentially a perfect storm and a rare occurrence. It's like a miracle that they ever form." The professor elaborates: "Corundum is rare, the elemental substitutions are rare, chromium itself is rare, and even *more* rare is the fact that this cannot occur in the presence of silica or large amounts of iron, and silica is one of the most abundant elements in the crust and iron is common too but must be in very low concentrations to form rubies. This can kind of be visualized as hmmm...like a Venn diagram of increasingly more rare occurrences and just a tiny overlapped center where the formation of this gemstone is actually possible."

22. C: The professor states: "Rubies are a specific type of the rare mineral corundum, which is composed of densely packed aluminum and oxygen atoms. These atoms are normally colorless, but when other atoms, like in this case chromium, are substituted for a some of the uh...aluminum ones, the deep red color of rubies is produced. Other substitutions cause the bright colors of other gemstones such as sapphire from the substitution of um, uh...from titanium and iron." These means that gemstones get their colors via the various elemental substitutions to the normal arrangement of aluminum and oxygen atoms.

23. D: Listeners should recall that the professor says the following: "Scientists typically only address one question at a time so that they can use the scientific method...By focusing on just one hypothesis, scientists should only manipulate a single variable at a time, called the independent variable, and then examine its results on the dependent variable." Using this information, test takers can review the

proposed experiments in the answer choices and select the one that only manipulates one variable at a time, which is Choice *D:* An experiment that uses the same exact recipe but bakes them for different lengths of time. The other experiments were changing multiple factors at one time, which contradicts the premise of the scientific method.

24. A: According to the lecture, rubies are formed at the boundaries of different plates, such as in the Himalayas, where sedimentary rock gets pushed under the other plate and gets metamorphosed. Choice *C* is wrong because although they are found near the Himalayas, they are not abundant. The whole lecture focuses on how rare they are, which is the opposite of abundant.

25. A & C: According to the discussion, rubies are gemstones and "are a specific type of the rare mineral corundum." Choice *B* is incorrect because they are not readily formed; in fact, they are rare. Choice *D* is incorrect because the professor says that "Geologist can even date the formation of these gemstones with the tectonic movements."

26. C: The student is having an issue with her bill. It is higher than she predicted. She starts the conversation by saying: "Hi. Is this the right place to ask about a problem with my bill?" Then she later says, "So, I received my bill for the semester and it says I owe $18000. I thought I had a scholarship so there's no way I can pay this bill."

27. A, B & C: The financial aid offer says, "if you qualify for additional financial aid, we can set up a package for you. Some students get additional scholarships based on financial need, or there are loans, and work-study opportunities."

28. D: The financial aid officer tells the student, "The financial aid office is open Monday through Friday 9-4 but we close every day at noon for an hour for lunch." Therefore, all of the other choices would not be a good time to get help at the office because it would be closed.

29. A, B, & C: The financial aid officer says, "I see the tuition bullied to your account is $8500. Your meal plan and housing in the dorms is $7,000 this semester and there is a technology fee and other posted fees including your parking permit totaling $2500." There is no mention of a specific activities fee (Choice *D*).

30. According to the advice from the financial aid officer, the necessary order is the following:

1	Register to fill out the FAFSA
2	Input prior year's tax information
3	Evaluate financial aid package
4	Apply for a campus job
5	Pay balance on the account
6	Register for classes

31. B: The student is most likely to apply for a job at the computer lab. Listeners can select this response based on the student's comment: "Back home I worked as a computer programmer at my mom's software company."

32. B: The main topic of the discussion between the professor and her students is the themes in *Gulliver's Travels.* They discuss the figurative, rather than literal, meaning in Swift's book, which makes Choice *C* incorrect. Choices *A* and *D* are not really discussed, and are certainly not the main focus.

33. D: When the professor says, "I want to dig deeper into this thought…" she is implying that she wants to explore this topic more. This is a figure of speech. She is not literally digging for something she buried, which may the other options incorrect.

34. B: The professor likely says, "Name-dropping is our modern equivalent to Gulliver's boasting about his close relationships with Kings and Queens" to help students understand things in the book by relating it to things they are familiar with. This will help the students understand something that may otherwise feel abstract or foreign. Name-dropping is a phrase used to refer to the act of casually mentioning famous people's names in conversation, as if indicating one has a personal connection or relationship to them, with the hope of impressing others. It isn't a way to remember names (Choice *A*) and doesn't' refer to forgetting names (Choice *C*). She is not directly showing empathy towards Gilliver, although she is saying his actions, even if in poor choice, are still something people do today.

35. B: The professor argues that the value of reading *Gulliver's Travels* is to consider human nature and its imperfections. She says, "Gulliver's Travels" can be read simply for entertainment value, but the true worth of Swift's story is his comment on human nature and its imperfections."

36. A: According to the participants in the discussion, Swift would disagree because he thinks humans are antisocial. Natasha says, "I think Swift would disagree (that humans are "social animals") because he kind of calls readers' attention to our own antisocial behaviors that we try to gloss over or ignore entirely to preserve our self-esteem."

Listening Transcripts

Passage #1: Conversation

Narrator: Listen to the following conversation between two students and then answer the following questions.

Male student: Hi Deborah, how did you do on the biology exam?

Female student: Pretty well! I got a 96. How about you?

Male student: Wow. I'm jealous. I got a 69. This stuff isn't making sense to me.

Female student: Oh no, I'm sorry to hear that, Greg. I could help you study if you'd like. I usually go to the library after my classes for a couple hours. We could work together on the practice questions and tackle this week's assignment if you want.

Male student: Actually, that would be great. Are you sure you don't mind?

Female student: No, not at all. I have to go to my economics class right now, but I'm usually at the library around 4:00pm. I sit in the back by the reference section. Do you know where the encyclopedias are?

Male student: Uh, to be honest, I've never been to the library here. I don't even know where on campus it is. Is it over by the dining hall on the main quad?

Female student: Oh wow! You've never been?! Where do you study? Yes, it's over next to the administration building on the main quad, directly across from the dining hall. You need to make sure you have your college ID with you to get in.

Male student: I haven't really gotten into a study rhythm yet this semester. That may be part of my problem. I guess I study in my room, when my roommate and I aren't playing video games, that is. I lost my ID at the basketball game last weekend. Do you know where I can get a new one?

Female student: Oh Greg! We need to get you organized. But yes, go to the administration building with another form of picture ID, and you'll need to pay a $15 replacement fee, and fill out a form.

Male student: Does a driver's license work?

Female student: Yes. Do you drive?

Male student: Yes, I have a Honda Civic parked over by my dorm. I go off campus a lot to buy things at the grocery store or to go to the movies.

Female student: That's awesome. I would love to get off campus once in a while and get a breath of "real-world" air, if you know what I mean.

Male student: Yeah, absolutely. Hey, how about I take you with me when I go shopping tomorrow afternoon in exchange for you tutoring me with the biology stuff?

Female student: Sounds perfect! Well, I've got to run to Economics class now. I'll see you at the library at 4:00pm. Let's just meet on the front steps and then we will go in together and find somewhere to work.

Passage #2: Lecture

Narrator: Listen to the following part of a lecture on Executive Functioning Disorder from a psychology class.

Male professor: Today, we are going to pick up where we left off last class talking about learning disabilities. Now, we will turn our attention to another common learning disability known as Executive Functioning Disorder. Some people um...equate executive function with the CEO of the brain because the role of executive function is to plan, organize, and manage tasks, processes, and deadlines. Let's see...essentially, it is the sum total of mental processes that enable an individual to connect his or her past experiences with current and future situations. Individuals with executive functioning disorder may struggle with time management, organization, planning and forethought, um...follow through, memory, prioritizing, and getting started on tasks, among other challenges. Many students with executive functioning difficulties also struggle to apply previously learned ideas and information to new concepts or to solve problems. They also may find analyzing ideas and identifying when and how to seek help to be a challenge. Let's see...heeding attention to and remembering details is also encumbered. These difficulties can greatly impact a child or adult in school, work, and even with daily tasks that involve time management or multiple steps. Uh...students may lack the ability to plan work or change their plans, wait to be called on or to hear directions before proceeding, manage their time and space, get started on projects, switch between tasks efficiently, ask for guidance when they are confused, memorize and especially retrieve things from their memory, and turn in assignments in a timely manner.

I know many of you have expressed an interest in teaching someday so uh...it's important to think about how this will affect students in your classrooms. Let's see...students may need accommodations for assessments and test taking. For example, they may be permitted to provide oral answers rather than circling or filling in bubbles or writing. They may be provided with the test format ahead of time so they can understand what will be asked of them and just focus on the content during studying. They may be allowed additional time during test taking or they may be provided with outlines of a lesson prior to sitting through it. This helps, uh...because then they only need to focus on listening rather than uh...writing and listening.

Now, there are also things that teachers can do. Because of the challenges planning and following steps, teachers are encouraged to uh...give step-by-step instructions that students should repeat back to demonstrate listening and understanding. Um, the number of steps should remain reasonable and simple instructions, uh like those given in written form, should be provided. Depending on the age of the students and their reading abilities, a written outline of the lesson and any directions can also be provided. This is particularly important to assist with note-taking during a lesson and uh...help key students into the main points versus the details. Using directed phrases like, "this is important because..." can also help students identify key points and begin making connections as to why something is important. Like in our class,

teachers should review prior material briefly before building upon it in the new lesson. To help keep students on task and meeting deadlines, teachers can provide daily to do checklists, encourage an assignment notebook that parents must review with their child. Lastly, to optimize success with assessments, teachers should explain what an ideal assignment or test looks like and provide a model.

While executive functioning issues alone can have a significant impact on an individual, I want you to think about how it often um...appears concurrently with other learning disorders like ADHD or dyslexia. Remember? We talked about these last class. This can make it, uh...especially challenging.

Passage #3: Lecture

Narrator: Listen to part of a lecture from astronomy class and then answer the questions.

Female Professor: We are continuing our discussion today of the history of astronomers from ancient times working up to the present day. So, remember, we are talking about the key contributors that have helped build our understanding of astronomy today. Let's pick up now with Nicolaus Copernicus. Copernicus, in many ways, can be thought of as the first in the modern astronomy scientists because he overturned the geocentric model of the solar system that had stood for over two thousand years, and instead, correctly (but shockingly at the time) suggested that the sun was the center of the solar system and the planets revolved around the sun. This was basically the birth of our present understanding of the solar system – the Heliocentric model. Before we go on, I want to remind you about the geocentric model we talked about last class. Remember, the ancient Greeks believed in a geocentric model of the universe, such that the planets and stars rotated around the central, stationary Earth. But Copernicus recognized that the uh...that the moon rotated around the Earth and that the Earth is just one of several planets revolving around the Sun. He also noted that the Sun is a star, the closest star, and other stars are much further away, that Earth rotates around its axis every day in addition to its yearly revolution, and that closer planets have shorter "years." Pretty important discoveries, huh?

Then we have Tycho Brahe. Now, Brahe was instrumental in determining the positions of fixed stars, unaided by telescopes, which were not yet invented. He made astronomical tools to help with mapping and understanding the "heavens" and the Solar System. He thought the Earth was not moving and that the Sun and Moon revolved around the stationary planet, so we know now that this part was off-base, but he's still a key player in our evolution.

Johannes Kepler was interested in math and astronomy and felt that geometric figures influenced the universe. He built upon Copernicus' heliocentric model and you've probably heard of his three Laws of Planetary Motion. The first law states that planetary orbits are elliptical, not circular, and the Sun is at one of the foci and not the center. The second law says that the planetary speed is faster near the sun and slower when it is more distant. The third law is somewhat similar. This one states that um...that the larger the orbit of a planet, the slower its average velocity.

Next, we have Galileo Galilei. That's a fun name to say. Well, Galileo made many advancements to our thinking and to our ability to make further discoveries, like he invented the telescope. He used it to observe sunspots and discovered that the lunar surface, like Earth, had mountains and valleys. Let's see...he also noted that the Milky Way galaxy had separate stars, he discovered moons around Jupiter, and designed instruments such a compass and this neat little calculating device. These discoveries helped prove the universe was dynamic and changing. Perhaps most importantly, he lay the foundations for scientific thought and process, the importance of logic and reason, and how to do experiments.

Lastly, Sir Isaac Newton. Remember, Newton was the one that proposed the three laws of motion that I'm sure you've heard in physics class: an object in motion stays in motion and an object at rest stays at rest unless acted on by an external force, force equals mass times acceleration, and every action has an equal and opposite reaction. He also proposed the Universal Law of Gravitation, which states that gravity is a force and that every object in the Universe is attracted to every other object. The magnitude of this force is directly proportional to the product of the masses of the objects and inversely proportional to the square of the distances between them.

Passage #4: Lecture and Discussion

Narrator: Listen to the following portion of a lecture and discussion from a geology class.

Male Professor: So now I want to turn our discussion to your homework assignment, Anne Sasso's article in *Discover* magazine called "The Geology of...Rubies." This article discussed how rubies are formed, why they have been so enamored throughout history, and what causes their brilliant red color, which, as I hope you read, is due to the ultraviolet light from the Sun causing the chromium in rubies to glow. Geologists are still searching for reasons as to how the existence of rubies came to be. Do you remember how Penn State University Geosciences professor Peter Heaney referred to rubies as a "minor geological miracle"? Can anyone tell me why Dr. Heaney says this?

Male student: Basically, he's saying um...that the formation of rubies is essentially a perfect storm and a rare occurrence. It's like a miracle that they ever form.

Male professor: Exactly, Xavier. Rubies are a specific type of the rare mineral corundum, which is composed of densely packed aluminum and oxygen atoms. These atoms are normally colorless, but when other atoms, like in this case chromium, are substituted for a some of the uh...aluminum ones, the deep red color of rubies is produced. Other substitutions cause the bright colors of other gemstones such as sapphire from the substitution of um, uh...from titanium and iron. Corundum is rare, the elemental substitutions are rare, chromium itself is rare, and even *more* rare is the fact that this cannot occur in the presence of silica or large amounts of iron, and silica is one of the most abundant elements in the crust and iron is common too but must be in very low concentrations to form rubies. This can kind of be visualized as hmmm...like a Venn diagram of increasingly more rare occurrences and just a tiny overlapped center where the formation of this geone is actually possible.

Does anyone remember from the article how rubies form?

Female student: Was that the part about how they are used for jewelry and even people centuries ago marveled at their beauty?

Professor: Well that's more about their importance or our interest in them. I'm looking for how they are created geologically.

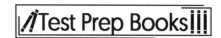

Female student: Oh! Oops. Yeah, they form through plate tectonics, particularly at the boundary by the um, um...Himalayas, where deposits of the sedimentary rock limestone get pushed under the other plate and metamorphosed into the marble.

Professor: Exactly Claudia! Molten granite in magma percolates in and infiltrates the forming marble. This limestone and granite interaction contains the chemical elements we now know are present in rubies. Importantly, this process removes the silica but left the aluminum. Geologist can even date the formation of these gemstones with the tectonic movements. Even more recently, teams of scientists have found that salt played an integral role in the formation of the rubies because it allowed the aluminum atoms to be fluid enough to get displaced occasionally by chromium.

Does anyone have any questions?... Yes, Xavier.

Male student: Have geologists done experiments to try to recreate all these conditions at once to make all different kinds of gemstones in the lab?

Professor: Well, kind of. Remember...scientists typically only address one question at a time so that they can use the scientific method. This method establishes a rigorous process of investigation so that it can be uh...replicated by other scientists to verify results. By focusing on just one hypothesis, scientists should only manipulate a single variable at a time, called the independent variable, and then examine its results on the dependent variable. What would happen if scientists didn't carefully isolate variables?

Female student: Well, if scientists were to manipulate multiple variables, it would be impossible to know which change resulted in the observed effects.

Professor: You got it! If scientists were to work to investigate multiple questions or change more than one variable when conducting an experiment, the research would be scattered, unfocused, and unable to prove anything.

Passage #5: Conversation

Narrator: Listen to the following conversation between a student and the school's financial aid officer.

Female student: Hi. Is this the right place to ask about a problem with my bill?

Male officer: Yes. This is the financial aid office so I can assist you with any tuition and billing questions.

Female student: Great. So, I received my bill for the semester and it says I owe $18000. I thought I had a scholarship so there's no way I can pay this bill, plus now there's a hold on my account so I can't seem to register for classes and I'm worried they are going to fill up.

Male officer: Ok let's see. Do you have a copy of your bill with you?

Female student: No. I left it in my dorm by accident.

Male officer: No problem. Can I see your student ID? I can pull it up in our system.

Female student: Yes. Here it is. Don't mind the picture. I didn't know I was going to be photographed that day!

Male officer: Oh, don't be silly…you look nice! Ok. Let me just take a look here at your bill and see what's going on. Hmm…Yes, I see the tuition billed to your account is $8500. Your meal plan and housing in the dorms is $7,000 this semester and there is a technology fee and other posted fees including your parking permit totaling $2500. The total amount posted to your account is $18000.

Female student: What about my scholarship?

Male officer: Well, it looks like you have a scholarship that is pending in your account for the amount of tuition, the $8500. It has not been applied because we are waiting on your financial aid application. Did you fill out the FAFSA? We need a current copy of that on file.

Female student: No. I didn't know I needed to do that.

Male officer: You'll definitely want to get that in as soon as possible. That way we can process your scholarship and also if you qualify for additional financial aid, we can set up a package for you. Some students get additional scholarships based on financial need, or there are loans, and work-study opportunities.

Female student: Oh, that sounds helpful. What is work-study?

Male officer: Work study refers to campus-based jobs where the compensation for you comes directly off of your bill. There are a variety of available positions for students around campus like in the library, at the sports center, or even in one of the administrative offices.

Female student: Ok cool. Back home I worked as a computer programmer at my mom's software company.

Male officer: Well we have lots of office positions too. So, what you need to do first is register to fill out FASFA on the website. You'll need to put in last year's tax information, so make sure you have that as well. Then, they will evaluate your financial aid package to determine what your needs are. If you want to do a work-study you can apply for a campus job. Lastly, make sure you pay the remaining balance on your account so that you can register for classes.

Female student: Ok thanks. I better get going on this!

Passage #6: Lecture Discussion

Narrator: Listen to the short lecture discussion in a literature class and then answer the questions.

Female professor: So, we've finally finished "Gulliver's Travels" by Jonathan Swift. As we've been discussing, this work is the expression of Swifts view of humanity hidden within the plot of a shipwrecked antihero's adventures. Gulliver is Swift's "everyman" and he represents, you know, like the English population in general. Although during his adventures Gulliver comments on the various creatures he encounters, those comments unknowingly reveal more information about Gulliver himself than their intended subjects. Through Gulliver, Swift argues that some of the forces that motivate human nature are quite unpleasant and embarrassing to admit.

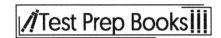

Why do you think Swift presents his argument about humankind this way? Through Gulliver as a vehicle, I mean?

Male student: Maybe because readers would otherwise deny these charges if Swift's argument wasn't presented in such a convincing manner?

Female professor: That's a great point, Alex. It helps the argument feel less personal as well. Swift shows how Gulliver's pride can take control of his actions and words. Gulliver cannot recognize his own faults even while notifying the reader of the same faults he sees in others. Remember how Swift shows Gulliver's tendency to lie, to project his self-hatred onto those around him, and to depend greatly on others to take care of him? Swift makes it clear that he views the general population to behave in much the same way. He suggests humans should behave more like the rational Houyhnhnm race created within the text. "Gulliver's Travels" can be read simply for entertainment value, but the true worth of Swift's story is his comment on human nature and its imperfections. Based on Swift's attitude as portrayed in this story, how do you think he'd respond to the fact that humans are often called "social animals"?

Female student: I think Swift would disagree because he kind of calls the readers' attention to our own antisocial behaviors that we try to gloss over or ignore entirely to preserve our self-esteem.

Female professor: Natasha, that's a fabulous point. One of Swift's prevailing opinions on human personality is that we are creatures driven by our excessive pride. Humans like to consider themselves to be more important than they actually are. Remember how Gulliver is always telling his readers that he was of the most importance to his various masters and their rulers? Like in Lilliput, the Imperial Majesty decides to have dinner with Gulliver. The rhetoric that Gulliver uses while relating this to the reader makes the occasion appear more momentous.

Female student: Yeah, he like glamorizes the situation and reveals that Gulliver considers himself to be of great concern to the powerful people of Lilliput.

Female Professor: Right! And his experiences in Brobdingnag include a similar occurrence. Hearing Gulliver tell us how important he is to the rulers of these foreign lands helps us realize how petty some of our own actions are. Name-dropping is our modern equivalent to Gulliver's boasting about his close relationships with Kings and Queens!

Male student: It seems Swift thinks that Humans are content to follow their mistakes through to the end rather than admit to making a mistake regardless of the consequences of unwavering persistence.

Professor: Wow, that's such a good point. What textual evidence do you have to support that thought?

Male student: Well, Gulliver stands by his convictions even after the reasonable king he respects greatly presents a profound argument against the usage of such a violent weapon.

Professor: I want to dig deeper into this thought but we have to end here today because of the time. Let's pick this back up on Thursday.

Speaking

The TOEFL Speaking Section assesses the test taker's ability to communicate effectively in English. This section lasts 20 minutes and test takers will encounter six tasks; the first two involve listening to brief recordings on familiar topics, and the remaining four ask test takers to read short passages, lectures, or conversations. For each task, test takers have about 15–30 seconds to gather their thoughts and prepare, and then they must deliver their verbal response into a microphone. The response is typically expected to last approximately 45 seconds, which can be nearly 100 words for a fluent English speaker. Test takers are evaluated on their oral delivery, topic development, content, language use, and grammar of their responses.

While this can sound daunting, the good news is that the Speaking section of the TOEFL is the easiest one to prepare for because the opportunities to practice are endless. Candidates should take advantage of every opportunity to practice their English-speaking skills, not only to optimize their test performance, but also because they will be frequently conversing in English in diverse situations long after passing the exam. Nearly every situation presents a valid opportunity to practice—driving the car, walking the dog, commuting to work, visiting a friend, doing errands, etc.

In addition to capitalizing on every chance to practice speaking, there are some other helpful strategies that successful test takers employ for this section.

Practice, but Don't Memorize

As mentioned, it's impossible to over-practice and the more speaking time a test taker has under his or her belt, the better. However, memorizing responses, particularly for the first two tasks (which tend to pose only a handful of possible questions), is not recommended. For one thing, scorers are looking for a natural speaking style that feels conversational and relaxed. Rehearsing and memorizing a predetermined response will likely lower one's delivery score even if the content is good. It is better to sound authentic and organic in the delivery of the answer, even if it means slightly less content is delivered in the allotted time.

Listen and Read the Question Carefully

It's easy to jump to an answer when nervous, but successful test takers make sure to pay careful attention to the specific question posed in the task and ensure that their response addresses the exact points desired. For example, the first task usually asks general questions such as what do you enjoy doing in your spare time, what is your family like, or what are your favorite places to visit? Test takers who are overly rehearsed may begin to hear a familiar prompt and then assume they know what the question is asking and prepare to deliver their memorized response. However, this hastiness can lead to mistakes; oftentimes, there are slight changes in the wording of the questions such that the exact question test administrators are looking for is different than that assumed. Instead of what do you enjoy doing on your spare time, the question may be more specific and ask, what do you enjoy doing by yourself in your spare time? If a test taker did not listen carefully or jumped to a prepared answer about enjoying basketball with his or her team or shopping with friends, points would be deducted for inappropriate content for the intended answer.

Organize

Test takers should take advantage of the 15–30 seconds provided to reflect on the question and organize their thoughts before they have to deliver their response. Many people find it helpful to write down a couple of bullet points that they plan to highlight in their answer. These should be just a word or short phrase, rather than a whole sentence, so as to save time and sound organic and natural in the response. Reading fully composed sentences tends to sound overly rehearsed and may affect one's delivery score.

Speak Clearly and Simply

Many test takers feel anxious or self-conscious about delivering their responses with as little influence of an accent as possible. The good news is that the TOEFL does not expect candidates to speak with any sort of "American" accent and scores are not influenced by the responder's accent one way or another. What is important is that the response is clear, audible, and comprehensible. After all, if scorers cannot hear or understand the recorded answer, they cannot award it with high marks. Test takers should speak as fluidly as possible, without rushing or interjecting long pauses or words of varying volumes. As much as possible, words should be enunciated with all syllables present and emphasizing those necessary for proper pronunciation. The more even and rhythmic the spoken answer, the better. One more point to note is that many test takers imagine that adding fancy vocabulary words will bolster their score. While demonstrating a rich vocabulary and strong command of English grammar and language skills is important, it is more important to ensure that words are used properly and that sentence structure and intended meaning is on point. If test takers are not confident in the meaning or proper usage of a word, it is better to use a seemingly simpler word whose meaning they are sure of.

Make Speech Flow

As mentioned, answers should flow as naturally fluidly as possible. With that said, short pauses should be interjected at the end of each sentence or where commas would be used in written text to help listeners understand the thoughts and the organization of the response. Rushing into each subsequent sentence without an adequate pause tends to make answers sound confusing. To connect thoughts together and create a logical flow to the response, test takers should demonstrate command of the use of conjunctions and employ effective connecting words and phrases such as: *because, due to, for example, after this, if…then,* and *however*.

Structure the Answer

Although spoken language is often not as formal as written communication, answers should still be organized, with well-developed thoughts presented in a logical order. Successful test takers generate their ideas and plan their delivery during the reflection time prior to recording their responses. It is wise to start the answer by stating the topic thought (like a topic sentence in a written essay) and then expand or describe that thought in the subsequent sentences. Adding a concluding sentence that ties back to the beginning thought gives the listener clarity and pulls all the details together into a comprehensive and intelligent answer.

Tell a Story

The most memorable conversations are those that include a captivating story. Speakers should try to make responses engaging and personal, when appropriate. This will not only make for a more enjoyable listen for scorers, but also can improve one's score by garnering more delivery points.

Be Confident

Everyone has important things to say. Test takers should not worry about saying something "stupid" or "boring." They should speak from the heart and be confident in their command of English as well as their comprehension of the posed question. There is no need to rush when delivering the response; there is plenty of time in 45 seconds to get out a complete answer. On that note, if there is extra time at the end of the allotted recording time, it is generally recommended to simply end the response when the question has been fully answered rather than fill every last second with speaking. It is unnecessary to speak aimlessly at the end, as this can reduce one's content score if the answer starts deviating from what was asked. Test takers should just pace themselves, stay relaxed, and speak with authority.

Practice Questions

1. Imagine that you are selected to be a tour guide for an exchange student for an afternoon. Talk about your favorite places in your city, town, or campus. Describe these places and explain why you like them.

   Preparation Time: 15 seconds
   Response Time: 45 seconds

2. Some people think it's smarter for people to set realistic goals that they are confident they can achieve, while others argue it's better to set ambitious goals that one may fail to achieve. What is your opinion? Explain why.

   Preparation Time: 15 seconds
   Response Time: 45 seconds

3. Read the following passage and then the conversation. Lastly, answer the question that follows them.

   The following text was reported by the University administrators to all students and their parents. Read the announcement. (The allotted reading time on the exam would be 45-60 seconds).

   Students are likely aware of the General Education requirements at the University. All students must take a handful of classes distributed across all major academic disciplines in addition to the specific course requirements dictated by their major. This design exposes students to a variety of fields in the social and physical sciences, the arts, and mathematics so that all of our graduates have a well-rounded liberal arts education in addition to the advanced studies in their field of choice. Upon reviewing the requirements and the surveys from our department heads about student benchmarks and achievements, the University's Academic Advisory Committee has decided to implement an additional writing requirement. This decision was based on the collective feeling among faculty members that the ability to communicate effectively in an academic tone is paramount to students' future career success. Beginning in the next academic year, in addition to the writing requirement that freshmen must satisfy, all students must take an additional academic writing course during their degree program. This new policy will apply to all current and incoming students.

   Female student: I think the Academic Advisory Committee has made a bad decision. I'm mad.

   Male student: Really? Why do you think it's a bad decision?

   Female student: We already have to take a bunch of distribution requirements and they're boring. If we know what we want to study, why should we have to take courses in other departments?

   Male student: Well, I think some students haven't fully decided what they want to major in, so the general education requirements expose them to all sorts of topics, so they can think about different careers, maybe even ones they didn't consider.

   Female student: Yeah, but they are free to dabble in whatever. I've known I want to major in biology and do the pre-med track since I was young. I've always wanted to be a doctor. The last thing I need is another writing class!

   Male student: I see your point but the ability to write well is so important in all fields, even medicine. Imagine if you conduct important research that will help patients improve their health. If you are unable to communicate it effectively and professionally in writing, your research won't be published and the patients won't benefit from your work.

Female student: I think that's a stretch. We have been writing our whole lives and the one freshmen writing class requirement is plenty. There's no way we need a whole additional writing course to be decent academic writers. It's a waste of time and we'd be better suited to take another class in our major that we're actually interested in.

Question: *The female student expresses her opinion of the University's new writing requirement. State and explain her opinion and compare it with the* Academic Advisory Committee's opinion.

Preparation Time: 30 seconds
Response Time: 60 seconds

4. Read the passage from a sports psychology textbook and the lecture that follows it. Then, answer the question. (Reading time in an actual test would be 45-50 seconds.)

The Inverted-U Theory of Arousal

The Inverted-U Theory posits that too little or too much arousal negatively impacts athletic performance, and there is an optimal level of arousal that facilitates optimal performance. The inverted-U graphically shows this (x-axis is level of arousal; y-axis is performance), as the shape demonstrates that low levels or high levels beyond the optimal level of arousal result in worse performance, and somewhere between low and high arousal is the range of arousal associated with optimal performance (the top of the inverted-U). At this point, the internal and external stimuli experienced by the athlete generate the optimal amount of arousal required to enhance performance. Some anticipation, anxiety, and arousal leads to increased levels of epinephrine, which prepares the body for increased athletic performance. On the other hand, too much stress and arousal can flood the system with epinephrine and increase heart rate and blood pressure beyond helpful levels. This can lead to a detrimental state where the exercise, on top of the increased sympathetic nervous system response, drives these physiologic variables too high, resulting in the body reducing its physical output during the exercise.

Professor: Arousal is an important concept in sports psychology and there several theories that have been developed to model the optimal arousal for performance. As your textbook mentions, the "inverted U" visually shows the optimal point on the arousal-relaxation curve, for best performance. For example, if an athlete is too relaxed and unfocused, his or her heart rate will be slow and the body will not be ready to perform well athletically. These athletes may need cheering, motivation, verbal "pumping up," and some small stimulus of external pressure to increase their arousal. I used to coach an athlete that was overly anxious. She would get so worked up before basketball games that her heart would be racing, her palms would be sweaty, and she would start to fatigue before the game even started, which negatively impacted her performance. She sometimes was so jittery that she missed easy shots and could barely run down the court without being winded.

Question: Explain the Inverted-U Theory and how the professor's example illustrates how the concept can be applied.

Preparation Time: 30 seconds
Response Time: 60 seconds

5. Read the conversation between two students and then answer the question that follows.

Female student: Hi Charlie, how are you liking your classes so far?

Male student: I like them a lot but I'm already falling behind because I don't have the textbooks yet.

Female student: Oh no! Have you not had a chance to go to the University bookstore to buy them?

Male student: Well, it's not that. It's just that I don't know if I want to buy them there new or rent them online.

Female student: You can rent textbooks?

Male student: Yeah. Basically, you pay less money and it's a digital subscription to the book for the duration of the semester, after which the book isn't available to you anymore. I've never done it before but it's much less expensive than buying them at the bookstore.

Female student: That's interesting but then you don't get to keep the book. What if you want to refer back to it in subsequent courses and semesters?

Male student: Yeah, then you don't have it anymore but buying books new is so expensive and honestly, I rarely use them again once the course is over. I mean, especially for classes outside of my major!

Female student: That's true and they do take up a lot of room. Plus, they're heavy. My back hates me every time I tote them around. Since the rented ones are digital e-books, you don't have the weight.

Male student: Exactly! I hate lugging them around and I like reading on my tablet in bed, and this way I could just read them more comfortably. The one thing is that you can't highlight them. I like the highlight as I read instead of taking notes. I can't really do that if I don't have a physical textbook.

Female student: Those are good points. Well, Charlie, I'd decide soon because either way, you'll want to get books soon so that you don't fall behind in class!

Male student: Yeah, you're right Martina. I'll think about it.

Question: Briefly summarize Charlie's problem and the two options. Then, state which solution you would recommend. Be sure to explain the reasons for your recommendation.

Preparation Time: 20 seconds
Response Time: 60 seconds

6. Read part of a lecture in an earth science course and then answer the question that follows.

Female Professor: Minor members of the solar system are those objects that are too small to be classified as planets, yet in aggregate, they make up a large percentage of the "stuff" in our solar system. Asteroids, meteors, and comets are examples of minor members. In addition to being smaller than planets, asteroids and comets have more irregular orbits and can even enter the Earth's atmosphere and collisions with Earth, the moon, the Sun, or other planets.

Some people theorize that the main asteroids, which lie in a tight belt between Mars and Jupiter, may all be fragments from another planet that was forming there that suffered some sort of major collision and broke into thousands of little pieces. Comets tend to be more scattered and found in the far-reaching edges of the Solar System. However, both of these minor bodies are subject to changes in gravitational pulls or perturbations, which can alter their trajectories and cause various collisions and changes in course.

Generally speaking, comets are smaller than asteroids and are not as confined to a particular region. They also tend to be more elliptical in shape and have chemical components that vaporize when heated, perhaps because they contain more ice than asteroids, which are mostly composed of chunks of rock. Some people describe them as "fuzzy looking," when observed through a telescope because they grow tails as a function of their elliptical orbit that the sun illuminates. Comets are not always visible in the night sky, although they sometimes streak across in bright glows, such as Halley's comet. Because of the irregularity of their orbits, they are subject to impacts with Earth. Astronomers also believe that there is a concentration of comets near Neptune in what is called the Kuiper belt. Asteroids also can enter our atmosphere but many are quite small and burn up in the atmosphere on their way down. It is theorized that such a collision from a massive asteroid caused the extinction of the dinosaurs.

Question: Using points and information from the lecture, describe the two different examples of minor members of the Solar System detailed by the professor.

Preparation Time: 20 seconds
Response Time: 60 seconds

Sample Answers

1. I live in New York City and I love it here. There are a lot of interesting places where I would enjoy taking an exchange student. I think I would choose sites that are less well-known, because they attract fewer tourists and are less crowded. General Grant's tomb is situated next to Riverside Park and has beautiful views of the Hudson river and George Washington Bridge. The architecture of the tomb and the bridge are striking and it is very lovely walking along the pathways. There is an interesting museum dedicated to this history of General Grant and New York City there as well. I would also take the student to the Natural History Museum, which is on the west side of Central Park. Although this museum does attract a lot of tourists, it does rightfully so because it has a fascinating collection of rocks, minerals, historic natural specimens, and exhibits about animals, biomes, and the evolution of different cultures and societies. I saw a fantastic exhibit about the biodiversity and ecology of Cuba and saw an interesting planetarium show about the night sky. Nearby, there is a great rooftop bar where you can enjoy drinks and appetizers in the open air above the city.

2. I think it is better to set ambitious goals even if there is a chance of failure. When people set goals that are too easy, they are denying themselves the chance to really push themselves and grow. If someone doesn't set their sights high and just stays within their comfort zone, they'll never know what they can achieve and they might limit their potential. If instead, they set a big, lofty goal, they may fall short and not fully achieve it but they will likely still exceed where they would have landed with a low-level goal. For example, if an athlete wants to run a 5k race and get a fast time, she will be motivated to train really hard and stay disciplined if she sets a big goal that excites her. If she sets an easy goal that she is pretty confident she can achieve without putting in much work, she will probably not push herself as hard in workouts and might get a slower time.

3. The female student thinks that the new additional writing course requirement at the University is unnecessary and she's not happy about the Academic Advisory Committee's decision to implement it. She thinks that because college students have been writing their whole lives, the one freshmen writing class requirement they already have is plenty. She thinks any additional writing class would be a waste of time, especially for students who know what they want to study. Those students would do better taking an additional course in their major, particularly if their focus doesn't relate too directly to writing, in her opinion. The University's Academic Advisory Committee, on the other hand, has implemented the additional writing course because the University's faculty feels that students' ability to communicate effectively in an academic tone is critical for future success in jobs and life.

4. The Inverted-U Theory is used in sports psychology to describe ideal levels of arousal for optimal athletic performance. The theory gets its name from its characteristic shape. It is graphed as an upside-down 'U" with arousal versus performance. Being too relaxed or too stressed about an athletic event can be detrimental to performance because the body reacts physiologically to the stress itself, by influencing heart rate and levels of hormones, like epinephrine. Instead, being moderately stressed and somewhat relaxed at the same time is ideal for success. The professor talks about the anxious basketball player he coached. She would get so wound up for games that she would get winded and tired, miss easy shots, and play worse. As a coach, he could apply this concepts of the Inverted-U Theory by working with the athlete on meditation and relaxation exercises in practices and games so help calm her down before she would need to play. This could help prevent her from getting overly anxious and keep her more in the optimal level. This is the opposite approach that he'd have to take with overly relaxed athletes. He mentioned that these athletes may need cheering or pumping up, and a little bit of pressure to bring them up to more ideal levels of arousal for success.

5. Charlie needs to purchase textbooks for his courses but he's not sure whether to buy physical books from the University bookstore or rent digital textbooks online. The digital books are much less expensive than the bookstore books and they obviously don't have the weight and bulk of real books. However, students don't get to keep them after the term, which may be an issue if they want to refer back to them and they can't highlight them as they study. I would recommend that he buy physical textbooks for those classes that he's taking in his major and rent the digital books for classes he has to take for general education classes outside of his major. That way, he'll save some money by buying fewer physical books with the cheaper e-textbooks, but he'll have the hard copy books for classes in his major in case he wants to look back on them in future classes and he can highlight them while he's reading to make sure he's really understanding the material as he studies, which is very important for classes in his major.

6. This lecture described asteroids and comets, which are both minor members of the Solar System. This means that they are smaller than planets. Both asteroids and comets have more irregular orbits than the planets and they can enter the atmosphere and collide with the moon, Sun, Earth or other planets. In fact, it was likely an asteroid collision that caused the extinction of the dinosaurs! Scientists think asteroids and comets are ice and rock remains from when the planets formed during the Big Bang. Asteroids are mostly concentrated in one area between Mars and Jupiter, while comets tend to be more scattered throughout the Solar System and some are much further away. Comets are usually smaller than asteroids, more elliptical instead of round, and have tails, which make them look fuzzy when viewed through a microscope. They can streak across the sky. Asteroids are made of less ice and more rock than comets. Many small ones enter our atmosphere but they burn up before reaching the surface of the Earth.

Writing

The TOEFL writing section consists of two different writing questions. The first writing section gives you a passage to read about a topic. Then, you will listen to a short lecture around two minutes long over the same topic. Though the two different mediums are over the same topic, they may have differing opinions. You will then have twenty minutes to write an essay synthesizing the two pieces.

The second writing section consists of a single prompt. You will have thirty minutes to complete this prompt, and you should plan on writing at least 300 words. The question of this essay is usually in one of the following structures:

- Your opinion on an issue
- Do you agree or disagree?
- Which would you prefer?
- Do you support or oppose this idea?
- Use specific reasons and examples

Writing the Essay

Brainstorming

One of the most important steps in writing an essay is prewriting. Before drafting an essay, it's helpful to think about the topic for a moment or two, in order to gain a more solid understanding of what the task is. Then, spending about five minutes jotting down the immediate ideas that could work for the essay is recommended. It is a way to get some words on the page and offer a reference for ideas when drafting. Scratch paper is provided for writers to use any prewriting techniques such as webbing, free writing, or listing. The goal is to get ideas out of the mind and onto the page.

Considering Opposing Viewpoints

In the planning stage, it's important to consider all aspects of the topic, including different viewpoints on the subject. There are more than two ways to look at a topic, and a strong argument considers those opposing viewpoints. Considering opposing viewpoints can help writers present a fair, balanced, and informed essay that shows consideration for all readers. This approach can also strengthen an argument by recognizing and potentially refuting the opposing viewpoint(s).

Drawing from personal experience may help to support ideas. For example, if the goal for writing is a personal narrative, then the story should be from the writer's own life. Many writers find it helpful to draw from personal experience, even in an essay that is not strictly narrative. Personal anecdotes or short stories can help to illustrate a point in other types of essays as well.

Moving from Brainstorming to Planning

Once the ideas are on the page, it's time to turn them into a solid plan for the essay. The best ideas from the brainstorming results can then be developed into a more formal outline. An outline typically has one main point (the thesis) and at least three sub-points that support the main point. Here's an example:

Main Idea

- Point #1
- Point #2
- Point #3

Of course, there will be details under each point, but this approach is the best for dealing with timed writing.

Staying on Track

Basing the essay on the outline aids in both organization and coherence. The goal is to ensure that there is enough time to develop each sub-point in the essay, roughly spending an equal amount of time on each idea. Keeping an eye on the time will help. If there are fifteen minutes left to draft the essay, then it makes sense to spend about 5 minutes on each of the ideas. Staying on task is critical to success and timing out the parts of the essay can help writers avoid feeling overwhelmed.

Parts of the Essay

The **introduction** has to do a few important things:

- Establish the **topic** of the essay in original wording (i.e., not just repeating the prompt)
- Clarify the significance/importance of the topic or purpose for writing (not too many details, a brief overview)
- Offer a **thesis statement** that identifies the writer's own viewpoint on the topic (typically one to two brief sentences as a clear, concise explanation of the main point on the topic)

Body paragraphs reflect the ideas developed in the outline. Three to four points is probably sufficient for a short essay, and they should include the following:

- A **topic sentence** that identifies the sub-point (e.g., a reason why, a way how, a cause or effect)
- A detailed **explanation** of the point, explaining why the writer thinks this point is valid
- Illustrative **examples**, such as personal examples or real-world examples, that support and validate the point (i.e., "prove" the point)
- A **concluding sentence** that connects the examples, reasoning, and analysis to the point being made

The **conclusion**, or final paragraph, should be brief and should reiterate the focus, clarifying why the discussion is significant or important. It is important to avoid adding specific details or new ideas to this paragraph. The purpose of the conclusion is to sum up what has been said to bring the discussion to a close.

Don't Panic!

Writing an essay can be overwhelming, and performance panic is a natural response. The outline serves as a basis for the writing and helps writers keep focused. Getting stuck can also happen, and it's helpful

to remember that brainstorming can be done at any time during the writing process. Following the steps of the writing process is the best defense against writer's block.

Timed essays can be particularly stressful, but assessors are trained to recognize the necessary planning and thinking for these timed efforts. Using the plan above and sticking to it helps with time management. Timing each part of the process helps writers stay on track. Sometimes writers try to cover too much in their essays. If time seems to be running out, this is an opportunity to determine whether all of the ideas in the outline are necessary. Three body paragraphs are sufficient, and more than that is probably too much to cover in a short essay.

More isn't always *better* in writing. A strong essay will be clear and concise. It will avoid unnecessary or repetitive details. It is better to have a concise, five-paragraph essay that makes a clear point, than a ten-paragraph essay that doesn't. The goal is to write one to two pages of quality writing. Paragraphs should also reflect balance; if the introduction goes to the bottom of the first page, the writing may be going off-track or be repetitive. It's best to fall into the one to two-page range, but a complete, well-developed essay is the ultimate goal.

The Final Steps

Leaving a few minutes at the end to revise and proofread offers an opportunity for writers to polish things up. Putting one's self in the reader's shoes and focusing on what the essay actually says helps writers identify problems—it's a movement from the mindset of writer to the mindset of editor. The goal is to have a clean, clear copy of the essay. The following areas should be considered when proofreading:

- Sentence fragments
- Awkward sentence structure
- Run-on sentences
- Incorrect word choice
- Grammatical agreement errors
- Spelling errors
- Punctuation errors
- Capitalization errors

The Short Overview

The essay may seem challenging, but following these steps can help writers focus:

- Take one to two minutes to think about the topic.
- Generate some ideas through brainstorming (three to four minutes).
- Organize ideas into a brief outline, selecting just three to four main points to cover in the essay (eventually the body paragraphs).
- Develop essay in parts:
- Introduction paragraph, with intro to topic and main points
- Viewpoint on the subject at the end of the introduction
- Body paragraphs, based on outline
- Each paragraph: makes a main point, explains the viewpoint, uses examples to support the point
- Brief conclusion highlighting the main points and closing
- Read over the essay (last five minutes).
- Look for any obvious errors, making sure that the writing makes sense.

Parts of Speech

Nouns

A **common noun** is a word that identifies any of a class of people, places, or things. Examples include numbers, objects, animals, feelings, concepts, qualities, and actions. *A, an,* or *the* usually precedes the common noun. These parts of speech are called *articles*. Here are some examples of sentences using nouns preceded by articles.

> *A* building is under construction.

> *The* girl would like to move to *the* city.

A **proper noun** (also called a **proper name**) is used for the specific name of an individual person, place, or organization. The first letter in a proper noun is capitalized. "My name is *Mary.*" "I work for *Walmart.*"

Nouns sometimes serve as adjectives (which themselves describe nouns), such as "hockey player" and "state government."

Pronouns

A word used in place of a noun is known as a **pronoun.** Pronouns are words like *I, mine, hers,* and *us.*

Pronouns can be split into different classifications (as shown below) which make them easier to learn; however, it's not important to memorize the classifications.

- **Personal pronouns:** refer to people

- **First person pronouns:** we, I, our, mine

- **Second person pronouns:** you, yours

- **Third person pronouns:** he, she, they, them, it

- **Possessive pronouns:** demonstrate ownership (mine, his, hers, its, ours, theirs, yours)

- **Interrogative pronouns:** ask questions (what, which, who, whom, whose)

- **Relative pronouns:** include the five interrogative pronouns and others that are relative (whoever, whomever, that, when, where)

- **Demonstrative pronouns:** replace something specific (this, that, those, these)

- **Reciprocal pronouns:** indicate something was done or given in return (each other, one another)

- **Indefinite pronouns:** have a nonspecific status (anybody, whoever, someone, everybody, somebody)

Indefinite pronouns such as *anybody, whoever, someone, everybody,* and *somebody* command a singular verb form, but others such as *all, none,* and *some* could require a singular or plural verb form.

Antecedents

An **antecedent** is the noun to which a pronoun refers; it needs to be written or spoken before the pronoun is used. For many pronouns, antecedents are imperative for clarity. In particular, a lot of the personal, possessive, and demonstrative pronouns need antecedents. Otherwise, it would be unclear who or what someone is referring to when they use a pronoun like *he* or *this*.

Pronoun reference means that the pronoun should refer clearly to one, clear, unmistakable noun (the antecedent).

Pronoun-antecedent agreement refers to the need for the antecedent and the corresponding pronoun to agree in gender, person, and number. Here are some examples:

> The *kidneys* (plural antecedent) are part of the urinary system. *They* (plural pronoun) serve several roles.

> The kidneys are part of the *urinary system* (singular antecedent). *It* (singular pronoun) is also known as the renal system.

Pronoun Cases

The **subjective pronouns** —*I, you, he/she/it, we, they,* and *who*—are the subjects of the sentence.

> Example: *They* have a new house.

The **objective pronouns**—*me, you* (*singular*), *him/her, us, them,* and *whom*—are used when something is being done for or given to someone; they are objects of the action.

> Example: The teacher has an apple for *us*.

The **possessive pronouns**—*mine, my, your, yours, his, hers, its, their, theirs, our,* and *ours*—are used to denote that something (or someone) belongs to someone (or something).

> Example: It's *their* chocolate cake.

> Even Better Example: It's *my* chocolate cake!

One of the greatest challenges and worst abuses of pronouns concerns *who* and *whom*. Just knowing the following rule can eliminate confusion. *Who* is a subjective-case pronoun used only as a subject or subject complement. *Whom* is only objective-case and, therefore, the object of the verb or preposition.

> *Who* is going to the concert?

> You are going to the concert with *whom*?

Hint: When using *who* or *whom*, think of whether someone would say *he* or *him*. If the answer is *he*, use *who*. If the answer is *him*, use *whom*. This trick is easy to remember because *he* and *who* both end in vowels, and *him* and *whom* both end in the letter *M*.

Many possessive pronouns sound like contractions. For example, many people get *it's* and *its* confused. The word *it's* is the contraction for *it is*. The word *its* without an apostrophe is the possessive form of *it*.

>   I love that wooden desk. It's beautiful. (contraction)

>   I love that wooden desk. Its glossy finish is beautiful. (possessive)

If you are not sure which version to use, replace *it's/its* with *it is* and see if that sounds correct. If so, use the contraction (*it's*). That trick also works for *who's/whose, you're/your,* and *they're/their*.

Adjectives

"The *extraordinary* brain is the *main* organ of the central nervous system." The adjective *extraordinary* describes the brain in a way that causes one to realize it is more exceptional than some of the other organs while the adjective *main* defines the brain's importance in its system.

An **adjective** is a word or phrase that names an attribute that describes or clarifies a noun or pronoun. This helps the reader visualize and understand the characteristics—size, shape, age, color, origin, etc.— of a person, place, or thing that otherwise might not be known. Adjectives breathe life, color, and depth into the subjects they define. Life would be *drab* and *colorless* without adjectives!

Adjectives often precede the nouns they describe.

>   *She drove her <u>new</u> car.*

However, adjectives can also come later in the sentence.

>   *Her car is <u>new</u>.*

Adjectives using the prefix *a–* can only be used after a verb.

>   Correct: The dog was alive until the car ran up on the curb and hit him.

>   Incorrect: The alive dog was hit by a car that ran up on the curb.

Other examples of this rule include *awake, ablaze, ajar, alike,* and *asleep*.

Other adjectives used after verbs concern states of health.

>   The girl was finally *well* after a long bout of pneumonia.

>   The boy was *fine* after the accident.

An adjective phrase is not a bunch of adjectives strung together, but a group of words that describes a noun or pronoun and, thus, functions as an adjective. Very happy is an adjective phrase; so are way too hungry and passionate about traveling.

Possessives

In grammar, *possessive nouns* show ownership, which was seen in previous examples like *mine, yours,* and *theirs*.

Singular nouns are generally made possessive with an apostrophe and an *s* (*'s*).

> My *uncle's* new car is silver.

> The *dog's* bowl is empty.

> *James's* ties are becoming outdated.

Plural nouns ending in *s* are generally made possessive by just adding an apostrophe ('):

> The pistachio nuts' saltiness is added during roasting. (The saltiness of pistachio nuts is added during roasting.)

> The students' achievement tests are difficult. (The achievement tests of the students are difficult.)

If the plural noun does not end in an *s* such as *women,* then it is made possessive by adding an *apostrophe s* (*'s*)—*women's*.

Indefinite possessive pronouns such as *nobody* or *someone* become possessive by adding an *apostrophe s— nobody's* or *someone's*.

Verbs

The **verb** is the part of speech that describes an action, state of being, or occurrence.

A verb forms the main part of a predicate of a sentence. This means that the verb explains what the noun (which will be discussed shortly) is doing. A simple example is *time <u>flies</u>*. The verb *flies* explains what the action of the noun, *time*, is doing. This example is a *main* verb.

Helping (auxiliary) verbs are words like *have, do, be, can, may, should, must,* and *will.* "I *should* go to the store." Helping verbs assist main verbs in expressing tense, ability, possibility, permission, or obligation.

Particles are minor function words like *not, in, out, up,* or *down* that become part of the verb itself. "I might *not*."

Participles are words formed from verbs that are often used to modify a noun, noun phrase, verb, or verb phrase.

> The *running* teenager collided with the cyclist.

Participles can also create compound verb forms.

> He is *speaking*.

Verbs have five basic forms: the **base** form, the **-s** form, the **-ing** form, the **past** form, and the **past participle** form.

The past forms are either **regular** (*love/loved; hate/hated*) or **irregular** because they don't end by adding the common past tense suffix "-ed" (*go/went; fall/fell; set/set*).

Adverbs

Adverbs have more functions than adjectives because they modify or qualify verbs, adjectives, or other adverbs as well as word groups that express a relation of place, time, circumstance, or cause. Therefore, adverbs answer any of the following questions: *How, when, where, why, in what way, how often, how much, in what condition,* and/or *to what degree. How good looking is he? He is <u>very</u> handsome.*

Here are some examples of adverbs for different situations:

- how: quickly
- when: daily
- where: there
- in what way: easily
- how often: often
- how much: much
- in what condition: badly
- what degree: hardly

As one can see, for some reason, many adverbs end in *-ly*.

Adverbs do things like emphasize (*really, simply,* and *so*), amplify (*heartily, completely,* and *positively*), and tone down (*almost, somewhat,* and *mildly*).

Adverbs also come in phrases.

The dog ran as <u>though his life depended on it.</u>

Prepositions

Prepositions are connecting words and, while there are only about 150 of them, they are used more often than any other individual groups of words. They describe relationships between other words. They are placed before a noun or pronoun, forming a phrase that modifies another word in the sentence. **Prepositional phrases** begin with a preposition and end with a noun or pronoun, the **object of the preposition.** *A pristine lake is <u>near the store</u> and <u>behind the bank.</u>*

Some commonly used prepositions are *about, after, anti, around, as, at, behind, beside, by, for, from, in, into, of, off, on, to,* and *with.*

Complex prepositions, which also come before a noun or pronoun, consist of two or three words such as *according to, in regards to,* and *because of.*

Interjections

Interjections are words used to express emotion. Examples include *wow, ouch,* and *hooray.* Interjections are often separate from sentences; in those cases, the interjection is directly followed by an exclamation point. In other cases, the interjection is included in a sentence and followed by a comma. The punctuation plays a big role in the intensity of the emotion that the interjection is expressing. Using a comma or semicolon indicates less excitement than using an exclamation mark.

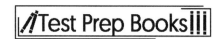

Conjunctions

Conjunctions are vital words that connect words, phrases, thoughts, and ideas. Conjunctions show relationships between components. There are two types:

Coordinating conjunctions are the primary class of conjunctions placed between words, phrases, clauses, and sentences that are of equal grammatical rank; the coordinating conjunctions are *for, and, nor, but, or, yet,* and *so.* A useful memorization trick is to remember that the first letter of these conjunctions collectively spell the word *fanboys.*

> I need to go shopping, *but* I must be careful to leave enough money in the bank.

> She wore a black, red, *and* white shirt.

Subordinating conjunctions are the secondary class of conjunctions. They connect two unequal parts, one **main** (or **independent**) and the other **subordinate** (or **dependent**). I must go to the store *even though* I do not have enough money in the bank.

> *Because* I read the review, I do not want to go to the movie.

Notice that the presence of subordinating conjunctions makes clauses dependent. *I read the review* is an independent clause, but *because* makes the clause dependent. Thus, it needs an independent clause to complete the sentence.

Sentences

First, let's review the basic elements of sentences.

A **sentence** is a set of words that make up a grammatical unit. The words must have certain elements and be spoken or written in a specific order to constitute a complete sentence that makes sense.

> 1. A sentence must have a **subject** (a noun or noun phrase). The subject tells whom or what the sentence is addressing (i.e. what it is about).

> 2. A sentence must have an **action** or **state of being** (*a* verb). To reiterate: A verb forms the main part of the predicate of a sentence. This means that it explains what the noun is doing.

> 3. A sentence must convey a complete thought.

When examining writing, be mindful of grammar, structure, spelling, and patterns. Sentences can come in varying sizes and shapes; so, the point of grammatical correctness is not to stamp out creativity or diversity in writing. Rather, grammatical correctness ensures that writing will be enjoyable and clear. One of the most common methods for catching errors is to mouth the words as you read them. Many typos are fixed automatically by our brain, but mouthing the words often circumvents this instinct and helps one read what's actually on the page. Often, grammar errors are caught not by memorization of grammar rules but by the training of one's mind to know whether something *sounds* right or not.

Types of Sentences

There isn't an overabundance of absolutes in grammar, but here is one: every sentence in the English language falls into one of four categories.

- Declarative: a simple statement that ends with a period

    The price of milk per gallon is the same as the price of gasoline.

- Imperative: a command, instruction, or request that ends with a period

    Buy milk when you stop to fill up your car with gas.

- Interrogative: a question that ends with a question mark

    Will you buy the milk?

- Exclamatory: a statement or command that expresses emotions like anger, urgency, or surprise and ends with an exclamation mark

    Buy the milk now!

Declarative sentences are the most common type, probably because they are comprised of the most general content, without any of the bells and whistles that the other three types contain. They are, simply, declarations or statements of any degree of seriousness, importance, or information.

Imperative sentences often seem to be missing a subject. The subject is there, though; it is just not visible or audible because it is *implied*. Look at the imperative example sentence.

    Buy the milk when you fill up your car with gas.

You is the implied subject, the one to whom the command is issued. This is sometimes called *the understood you* because it is understood that *you* is the subject of the sentence.

Interrogative sentences—those that ask questions—are defined as such from the idea of the word *interrogation*, the action of questions being asked of suspects by investigators. Although that is serious business, interrogative sentences apply to all kinds of questions.

To exclaim is at the root of **exclamatory sentences**. These are made with strong emotions behind them. The only technical difference between a declarative or imperative sentence and an exclamatory one is the exclamation mark at the end. The example declarative and imperative sentences can both become an exclamatory one simply by putting an exclamation mark at the end of the sentences.

    The price of milk per gallon is the same as the price of gasoline!
    Buy milk when you stop to fill up your car with gas!

After all, someone might be really excited by the price of gas or milk, or they could be mad at the person that will be buying the milk! However, as stated before, exclamation marks in abundance defeat their own purpose! After a while, they begin to cause fatigue! When used only for their intended purpose, they can have their expected and desired effect.

Independent and Dependent Clauses

Independent and dependent clauses are strings of words that contain both a subject and a verb. An **independent clause** *can* stand alone as complete thought, but a **dependent clause** *cannot*. A dependent clause relies on other words to be a complete sentence.

> Independent clause: The keys are on the counter.
> Dependent clause: If the keys are on the counter

Notice that both clauses have a subject (*keys*) and a verb (*are*). The independent clause expresses a complete thought, but the word *if* at the beginning of the dependent clause makes it *dependent* on other words to be a complete thought.

> Independent clause: If the keys are on the counter, please give them to me.

This presents a complete sentence since it includes at least one verb and one subject and is a complete thought. In this case, the independent clause has two subjects (*keys* & an implied *you*) and two verbs (*are* & *give*).

> Independent clause: I went to the store.
> Dependent clause: Because we are out of milk,

> Complete Sentence: Because we are out of milk, I went to the store.
> Complete Sentence: I went to the store because we are out of milk.

Sentence Structures

A **simple sentence** has one independent clause.

> I am going to win.

A **compound sentence** has two independent clauses. A conjunction—*for, and, nor, but, or, yet, so*—links them together. Note that each of the independent clauses has a subject and a verb.

> I am going to win, but the odds are against me.

A **complex sentence** has one independent clause and one or more dependent clauses.

> I am going to win, even though I don't deserve it.

Even though I don't deserve it is a dependent clause. It does not stand on its own. Some conjunctions that link an independent and a dependent clause are *although, because, before, after, that, when, which*, and *while*.

A **compound-complex sentence** has at least three clauses, two of which are independent and at least one that is a dependent clause.

> While trying to dance, I tripped over my partner's feet, but I regained my balance quickly.

The dependent clause is *While trying to dance*.

Run-Ons and Fragments

Run-Ons

A common mistake in writing is the run-on sentence. A **run-on** is created when two or more independent clauses are joined without the use of a conjunction, a semicolon, a colon, or a dash. We don't want to use commas where periods belong. Here is an example of a run-on sentence:

> Making wedding cakes can take many hours I am very impatient, I want to see them completed right away.

There are a variety of ways to correct a run-on sentence. The method you choose will depend on the context of the sentence and how it fits with neighboring sentences:

> Making wedding cakes can take many hours. I am very impatient. I want to see them completed right away. (Use periods to create more than one sentence.)

> Making wedding cakes can take many hours; I am very impatient—I want to see them completed right away. (Correct the sentence using a semicolon, colon, or dash.)

> Making wedding cakes can take many hours, and I am very impatient and want to see them completed right away. (Correct the sentence using coordinating conjunctions.)

> I am very impatient because I would rather see completed wedding cakes right away than wait for it to take many hours. (Correct the sentence by revising.)

Fragments

Remember that a complete sentence must have both a subject and a verb. Complete sentences consist of at least one independent clause. Incomplete sentences are called **sentence fragments**. A sentence fragment is a common error in writing. Sentence fragments can be independent clauses that start with subordinating words, such as *but, as, so that,* or *because,* or they could simply be missing a subject or verb.

You can correct a fragment error by adding the fragment to a nearby sentence or by adding or removing words to make it an independent clause. For example:

> Dogs are my favorite animals. Because cats are too lazy. (Incorrect; the word because creates a sentence fragment)

> Dogs are my favorite animals because cats are too lazy. (Correct; this is a dependent clause.)

> Dogs are my favorite animals. Cats are too lazy. (Correct; this is a simple sentence.)

Subject and Predicate

Every complete sentence can be divided into two parts: the subject and the predicate.

Subjects: We need to have subjects in our sentences to tell us who or what the sentence describes. Subjects can be simple or complete, and they can be direct or indirect. There can also be compound subjects.

Simple subjects are the noun or nouns the sentence describes, without modifiers. The simple subject can come before or after the verb in the sentence:

The big brown <u>dog</u> is the calmest one.

Complete subjects are the subject together with all of its describing words or modifiers.

The <u>big brown dog</u> is the calmest one. (The complete subject is big brown dog.)

Direct subjects are subjects that appear in the text of the sentence, as in the example above. **Indirect subjects** are implied. The subject is "you," but the word *you* does not appear.

Indirect subjects are usually in imperative sentences that issue a command or order:

Feed the short skinny dog first. (The understood you is the subject.)

Watch out—he's really hungry! (The sentence warns you to watch out.)

Compound subjects occur when two or more nouns join together to form a plural subject.

<u>Carson</u> and <u>Emily</u> make a great couple.

Predicates: Once we have identified the subject of the sentence, the rest of the sentence becomes the predicate. Predicates are formed by the verb, the direct object, and all words related to it.

We <u>went to see the Cirque du' Soleil performance</u>.

The gigantic green character <u>was funnier than all the rest</u>.

Direct objects are the nouns in the sentence that are receiving the action. Sentences don't necessarily need objects. Sentences only need a subject and a verb.

The clown brought the acrobat the <u>hula-hoop</u>. (What is getting brought? the hula-hoop)

Then he gave the trick pony a <u>soapy bath</u>. (What is being given? (a soapy bath)

Indirect objects are words that tell us to or for whom or what the action is being done. For there to be an indirect object, there first must always be a direct object.

The clown brought <u>the acrobat</u> the hula-hoop. (Who is getting the direct object? the hula-hoop)

Then he gave <u>the trick pony</u> a soapy bath. (What is getting the bath? a trick pony)

Phrases

A **phrase** is a group of words that go together but do not include both a subject and a verb. We use them to add information, explain something, or make the sentence easier for the reader to understand. Unlike clauses, phrases can never stand alone as their own sentence. They do not form complete thoughts. There are noun phrases, prepositional phrases, verbal phrases, appositive phrases, and absolute phrases. Here are some examples of phrases:

I know <u>all the shortest routes</u>.

<u>Before the sequel</u>, we wanted to watch the first movie. (introductory phrase)

The jumpers have hot cocoa <u>to drink right away</u>.

Subject-Verb Agreement

The subject of a sentence and its verb must agree. The cornerstone rule of subject-verb agreement is that subject and verb must agree in number. Whether the subject is singular or plural, the verb must follow suit.

Incorrect: The houses is new.

Correct: The houses are new.

Also Correct: The house is new.

In other words, a singular subject requires a singular verb; a plural subject requires a plural verb.

The words or phrases that come between the subject and verb do not alter this rule.

Incorrect: The houses built of brick is new.

Correct: The houses built of brick are new.

Incorrect: The houses with the sturdy porches is new.

Correct: The houses with the sturdy porches are new.

The subject will always follow the verb when a sentence begins with *here* or *there.* Identify these with care.

Incorrect: Here *is* the *houses* with sturdy porches.

Correct: Here *are* the *houses* with sturdy porches.

The subject in the sentences above is not *here*, it is *houses*. Remember, *here* and *there* are never subjects. Be careful that contractions such as *here's* or *there're* do not cause confusion!

Two subjects joined by *and* require a plural verb form, except when the two combine to make one thing:

Incorrect: Garrett and Jonathan is over there.

Correct: Garrett and Jonathan are over there.

Incorrect: Spaghetti and meatballs are a delicious meal!

Correct: Spaghetti and meatballs is a delicious meal!

In the example above, *spaghetti and meatballs* is a compound noun. However, *Garrett and Jonathan* is not a compound noun.

Two singular subjects joined by *or, either/or,* or *neither/nor* call for a singular verb form.

> Incorrect: Butter or syrup are acceptable.

> Correct: Butter or syrup is acceptable.

Plural subjects joined by *or, either/or,* or *neither/nor* are, indeed, plural.

The chairs or the boxes are being moved next.

If one subject is singular and the other is plural, the verb should agree with the closest noun.

> Correct: The chair or the boxes are being moved next.

> Correct: The chairs or the box is being moved next.

Some plurals of money, distance, and time call for a singular verb.

> Incorrect: Three dollars *are* enough to buy that.

> Correct: Three dollars *is* enough to buy that.

For words declaring degrees of quantity such as *many of, some of,* or *most of,* let the noun that follows *of* be the guide:

> Incorrect: Many of the books is in the shelf.

> Correct: Many of the books are in the shelf.

> Incorrect: Most of the pie *are* on the table.

> Correct: Most of the pie *is* on the table.

For indefinite pronouns like anybody or everybody, use singular verbs.

> Everybody *is* going to the store.

However, the pronouns *few, many, several, all, some,* and *both* have their own rules and use plural forms.

> Some *are* ready.

Some nouns like *crowd* and *congress* are called *collective nouns* and they require a singular verb form.

> Congress *is* in session.

> The news *is* over.

Books and movie titles, though, including plural nouns such as *Great Expectations*, also require a singular verb. Remember that only the subject affects the verb. While writing tricky subject-verb arrangements, say them aloud. Listen to them. Once the rules have been learned, one's ear will become sensitive to them, making it easier to pick out what's right and what's wrong.

Dangling and Misplaced Modifiers

A **modifier** is a word or phrase meant to describe or clarify another word in the sentence. When a sentence has a modifier but is missing the word it describes or clarifies, it's an error called a **dangling modifier**. We can fix the sentence by revising to include the word that is being modified. Consider the following examples with the modifier underlined:

Incorrect: Having walked five miles, this bench will be the place to rest. (This implies that the bench walked the miles, not the person.)

Correct: Having walked five miles, Matt will rest on this bench. (*Having walked five miles* correctly modifies *Matt*, who did the walking.)

Incorrect: Since midnight, my dreams have been pleasant and comforting. (The adverb clause *since midnight* cannot modify the noun *dreams*.)

Correct: Since midnight, I have had pleasant and comforting dreams. (*Since midnight* modifies the verb have had, telling us when the dreams occurred.)

Sometimes the modifier is not located close enough to the word it modifies for the sentence to be clearly understood. In this case, we call the error a **misplaced modifier**. Here is an example with the modifier underlined.

Incorrect: We gave the hot cocoa to the children that was filled with marshmallows. (This sentence implies that the children are what are filled with marshmallows.)

Correct: We gave the hot cocoa that was filled with marshmallows to the children. (The cocoa is filled with marshmallows. The modifier is near the word it modifies.)

Parallel Structure in a Sentence

Parallel structure, also known as **parallelism**, refers to using the same grammatical form within a sentence. This is important in lists and for other components of sentences.

Incorrect: At the recital, the boys and girls were dancing, singing, and played musical instruments.
Correct: At the recital, the boys and girls were dancing, singing, and playing musical instruments.

Notice that in the second example, *played* is not in the same verb tense as the other verbs nor is it compatible with the helping verb *were*. To test for parallel structure in lists, try reading each item as if it were the only item in the list.

The boys and girls were dancing.
The boys and girls were singing.
The boys and girls were played musical instruments.

Suddenly, the error in the sentence becomes very clear. Here's another example:

> Incorrect: After the accident, I informed the police *that Mrs. Holmes backed* into my car, *that Mrs. Holmes got out* of her car to look at the damage, and *she was driving* off without leaving a note.

> Correct: After the accident, I informed the police *that Mrs. Holmes backed* into my car, *that Mrs. Holmes got out* of her car to look at the damage, and *that Mrs. Holmes drove off* without leaving a note.

> Correct: After the accident, I informed the police that Mrs. Holmes *backed* into my car, *got out* of her car to look at the damage, and *drove off* without leaving a note.

Note that there are two ways to fix the nonparallel structure of the first sentence. The key to parallelism is consistent structure.

Punctuation

Commas

A **comma** (,) is the punctuation mark that signifies a pause—breath—between parts of a sentence. It denotes a break of flow. As with so many aspects of writing structure, authors will benefit by reading their writing aloud or mouthing the words. This can be particularly helpful if one is uncertain about whether the comma is needed.

In a complex sentence—one that contains a subordinate (dependent) clause or clauses—the use of a comma is dictated by where the subordinate clause is located. If the subordinate clause is located before the main clause, a comma is needed between the two clauses.

> I will not pay for the steak, *because I don't have that much money*.

Generally, if the subordinate clause is placed after the main clause, no punctuation is needed.

> I did well on my exam because I studied two hours the night before.

Notice how the last clause is dependent because it requires the earlier independent clauses to make sense.

Use a comma on both sides of an interrupting phrase.

> I will pay for the ice cream, *chocolate and vanilla*, and then will eat it all myself.

The words forming the phrase in italics are nonessential (extra) information. To determine if a phrase is nonessential, try reading the sentence without the phrase and see if it's still coherent.

A comma is not necessary in this next sentence because no interruption—nonessential or extra information—has occurred. Read sentences aloud when uncertain.

I will pay for his chocolate and vanilla ice cream and then will eat it all myself.

If the nonessential phrase comes at the beginning of a sentence, a comma should only go at the end of the phrase. If the phrase comes at the end of a sentence, a comma should only go at the beginning of the phrase.

Other types of interruptions include the following:

- interjections: Oh no, I am not going.
- abbreviations: Barry Potter, M.D., specializes in heart disorders.
- direct addresses: Yes, Claudia, I am tired and going to bed.
- parenthetical phrases: His wife, lovely as she was, was not helpful.
- transitional phrases: Also, it is not possible.

The second comma in the following sentence is called an Oxford comma.

> I will pay for ice cream, syrup, and pop.

It is a comma used after the second-to-last item in a series of three or more items. It comes before the word *or* or *and*. Not everyone uses the Oxford comma; it is optional, but many believe it is needed. The comma functions as a tool to reduce confusion in writing. So, if omitting the Oxford comma would cause confusion, then it's best to include it.

Commas are used in math to mark the place of thousands in numerals, breaking them up so they are easier to read. Other uses for commas are in dates (*March 19, 2016*), letter greetings (*Dear Sally,*), and in between cities and states (*Louisville, KY*).

Apostrophes

This punctuation mark, the apostrophe ('), is a versatile little mark. It has a few different functions:

- Quotes: Apostrophes are used when a second quote is needed within a quote.

- In my letter to my friend, I wrote, "The girl had to get a new purse, and guess what Mary did? She said, 'I'd like to go with you to the store.' I knew Mary would buy it for her."

- Contractions: Another use for an apostrophe in the quote above is a contraction. *I'd* is used for *I would.*

  The basic rule for making *contractions* is one area of spelling that is pretty straightforward: combine the two words by inserting an apostrophe (') in the space where a letter is omitted. For example, to combine *you* and *are*, drop the *a* and put the apostrophe in its place: *you're.*

  > he + is = he's

  > you + all = y'all (informal but often misspelled)

- Possession: An apostrophe followed by the letter *s* shows possession (*Mary's* purse). If the possessive word is plural, the apostrophe generally just follows the word.

- The trees' leaves are all over the ground.

Ellipses

An **ellipsis** (…) consists of three handy little dots that can speak volumes on behalf of irrelevant material. Writers use them in place of words, lines, phrases, list content, or paragraphs that might just as easily

have been omitted from a passage of writing. This can be done to save space or to focus only on the specifically relevant material.

> Exercise is good for some unexpected reasons. Watkins writes, "Exercise has many benefits such as...reducing cancer risk."

In the example above, the ellipsis takes the place of the other benefits of exercise that are more expected.

The ellipsis may also be used to show a pause in sentence flow.

> "I'm wondering...how this could happen," Dylan said in a soft voice.

Semicolons

The **semicolon** (;) might be described as a heavy-handed comma. Take a look at these two examples:

> I will pay for the ice cream, but I will not pay for the steak.
> I will pay for the ice cream; I will not pay for the steak.

What's the difference? The first example has a comma and a conjunction separating the two independent clauses. The second example does not have a conjunction, but there are two independent clauses in the sentence, so something more than a comma is required. In this case, a semicolon is used.

Two independent clauses can only be joined in a sentence by either a comma and conjunction or a semicolon. If one of those tools is not used, the sentence will be a run-on. Remember that while the clauses are independent, they need to be closely related in order to be contained in one sentence.

Another use for the semicolon is to separate items in a list when the items themselves require commas.

> The family lived in Phoenix, Arizona; Oklahoma City, Oklahoma; and Raleigh, North Carolina.

Colons

Colons (:) have many miscellaneous functions. Colons can be used to precede further information or a list. In these cases, a colon should only follow an independent clause.

> Humans take in sensory information through five basic senses: sight, hearing, smell, touch, and taste.

The meal includes the following components:

- Caesar salad
- spaghetti
- garlic bread
- cake

The family got what they needed: a reliable vehicle.

While a comma is more common, a colon can also proceed a formal quotation.

> He said to the crowd: "Let's begin!"

The colon is used after the greeting in a formal letter.

> Dear Sir:
> To Whom It May Concern:

In the writing of time, the colon separates the minutes from the hour (*4:45 p.m.*). The colon can also be used to indicate a ratio between two numbers (*50:1*).

Hyphens

The **hyphen** (-) is a little hash mark that can be used to join words to show that they are linked.

Hyphenate two words that work together as a single adjective (a compound adjective).

> honey-covered biscuits

Some words always require hyphens, even if not serving as an adjective.

> merry-go-round

Hyphens always go after certain prefixes like *anti-* & *all-*.

Hyphens should also be used when the absence of the hyphen would cause a strange vowel combination (*semi-engineer*) or confusion. For example, *re-collect* should be used to describe something being gathered twice rather than being written as *recollect*, which means to remember.

Parentheses and Dashes

Parentheses are half-round brackets that look like this: ( ). They set off a word, phrase, or sentence that is an afterthought, explanation, or side note relevant to the surrounding text but not essential. A pair of commas is often used to set off this sort of information, but parentheses are generally used for information that would not fit well within a sentence or that the writer deems not important enough to be structurally part of the sentence.

> The picture of the heart (see above) shows the major parts you should memorize.
> Mount Everest is one of three mountains in the world that are over 28,000 feet high (K2 and Kanchenjunga are the other two).

See how the sentences above are complete without the parenthetical statements? In the first example, *see above* would not have fit well within the flow of the sentence. The second parenthetical statement could have been a separate sentence, but the writer deemed the information not pertinent to the topic.

The **em-dash** (—) is a mark longer than a hyphen used as a punctuation mark in sentences and to set apart a relevant thought. Even after plucking out the line separated by the dash marks, the sentence will be intact and make sense.

> Looking out the airplane window at the landmarks—Lake Clarke, Thompson Community College, and the bridge—she couldn't help but feel excited to be home.

The dashes use is similar to that of parentheses or a pair of commas. So, what's the difference? Many believe that using dashes makes the clause within them stand out while using parentheses is subtler. It's advised to not use dashes when commas could be used instead.

Quotation Marks

Here are some instances where *quotation marks* should be used:

- Dialogue for characters in narratives. When characters speak, the first word should always be capitalized, and the punctuation goes inside the quotes. For example:

    Janie said, "The tree fell on my car during the hurricane."

- Around titles of songs, short stories, essays, and chapter in books
- To emphasize a certain word
- To refer to a word as the word itself

Capitalization

Here's a non-exhaustive list of things that should be capitalized.

- The first word of every sentence
- The first word of every line of poetry
- The first letter of proper nouns (World War II)
- Holidays (Valentine's Day)
- The days of the week and months of the year (Tuesday, March)
- The first word, last word, and all major words in the titles of books, movies, songs, and other creative works (In the novel, *To Kill a Mockingbird*, note that *a* is lowercase since it's not a major word, but *to* is capitalized since it's the first word of the title.)
- Titles when preceding a proper noun (President Roberto Gonzales, Aunt Judy)

When simply using a word such as president or secretary, though, the word is not capitalized.

    Officers of the new business must include a *president* and *treasurer*.

Seasons—spring, fall, etc.—are not capitalized.

North, *south*, *east*, and *west* are capitalized when referring to regions but are not when being used for directions. In general, if it's preceded by *the* it should be capitalized.

    I'm from the South.
    I drove south.

Word Confusion

That/Which

The pronouns *that* and *which* are both used to refer to animals, objects, ideas, and events—but they are not interchangeable. The rule is to use the word that in essential clauses and phrases that help convey the meaning of the sentence. Use the word *which* in nonessential (less important) clauses. Typically, *which* clauses are enclosed in commas.

    The morning <u>that I fell asleep in class</u> caused me a lot of trouble.

    This morning's coffee, <u>which had too much creamer</u>, woke me up.

Who/Whom

We use the pronouns *who* and *whom* to refer to people. We always use *who* when it is the subject of the sentence or clause. We never use *whom* as the subject; it is always the object of a verb or preposition.

Who hit the baseball for the home run? (subject)

The baseball fell into the glove of whom? (object of the preposition *of*)

The umpire called whom "out"? (object of the verb *called*)

To/Too/Two

to: a preposition or infinitive (*to walk, to run, walk to the store, run to the tree*)
too: means also, as well, or very (*She likes cookies, too.; I ate too much.*)
two: a number (*I have two cookies. She walked to the store two times.*)

There/Their/They're

there: an adjective, adverb, or pronoun used to start a sentence or indicate place (*There are four vintage cars over there.*)
their: a possessive pronoun used to indicate belonging (*Their car is the blue and white one.*)
they're: a contraction of the words "they are" (*They're going to enter the vintage car show.*)

Your/You're

your: a possessive pronoun (*Your artwork is terrific.*)
you're: a contraction of the words "you are" (*You're a terrific artist.*)

Its/It's

its: a possessive pronoun (*The elephant had its trunk in the water.*)
it's: a contraction of the words "it is" (*It's an impressive animal.*)

Affect/Effect

affect: as a verb means "to influence" (*How will the earthquake affect your home?*); as a noun means "emotion or mood" (*Her affect was somber.*)
effect: as a verb means "to bring about" (*She will effect a change through philanthropy.*); as a noun means "a result of" (*The effect of the earthquake was devastating.*)

Other mix-ups: Other pairs of words cause mix-ups but are not necessarily homonyms. Here are a few of those:

Bring/Take

bring: when the action is coming toward (*Bring me the money.*)
take: when the action is going away from (*Take her the money.*)

Can/May

can: means "able to" (*The child can ride a bike.*)
may: asks permission (*The child asked if he may ride his bike.*)

Than/Then

than: a conjunction used for comparison (*I like tacos better than pizza.*)
then: an adverb telling when something happened (*I ate and then slept.*)

Disinterested/Uninterested

disinterested: used to mean "neutral" (*The jury remains disinterested during the trial.*)
uninterested: used to mean "bored" (*I was uninterested during the lecture.*)

Percent/Percentage

percent: used when there is a number involved (*Five percent of us like tacos.*)
percentage: used when there is no number (*That is a low percentage.*)

Fewer/Less

fewer: used for things you can count (*He has fewer playing cards.*)
less: used for things you cannot count, as well as time (*He has less talent. You have less than a minute.*)

Farther/Further

farther: used when discussing distance (*His paper airplane flew farther than mine.*)
further: used to mean "more" (*He needed further information.*)

Lend/Loan

lend: a verb used for borrowing (*Lend me your lawn mower. He will lend it to me.*)
loan: a noun used for something borrowed (*She applied for a student loan.*)

Note

Some people have problems with these:

- regardless/irregardless
- a lot/alot

Irregardless and *alot* are always incorrect. Don't use them.

First Essay

1. First read the article below. Then click the link below the article and watch the Ted Talk video. Then review the prompt and write an essay synthesizing the two sources.

Caloric Intake From Fast Food Among Adults: United States, 2007-2010

by Cheryl D. Fryar, M.S.P.H., and R. Bethene Ervin, Ph.D., R.D.

Key findings

Data from the National Health and Nutrition Examination Survey

- During 2007–2010, adults consumed, on average, 11.3% of their total daily calories from fast food.

- The consumption of calories from fast food significantly decreased with age.

- Non-Hispanic black adults consumed a higher percentage of calories from fast food compared with non-Hispanic white and Hispanic adults.

- No difference was observed by income status in the percentage of calories consumed from fast food among all adults. Among young adults, however, as income increased, the percentage of calories from fast food decreased.

- The percentage of total daily calories from fast food increased as weight status increased.

As lifestyles become more hectic, fast-food consumption has become a growing part of the American diet (1,2). Fast food is food usually sold at eating establishments for quick availability or takeout (3). More than one-third of U.S. adults are obese (4), and frequent fast-food consumption has been shown to contribute to weight gain (1–6). This report presents the percentage of calories consumed from fast food by adults in the United States, including differences by sociodemographic characteristics and weight status.

What percentage of calories consumed by adults comes from fast food?

During 2007–2010, adults consumed an average 11.3% of their total daily calories from fast food (Figure 1), a decrease from 12.8% for 2003–2006 (data not shown). The percentage of calories consumed from fast food did not differ significantly between men (11.8%) and women (10.9%). The percentage of calories consumed from fast food decreased with age, with adults aged 60 and over (6.0%) consuming the lowest percentage of their daily calories from fast foods. This decrease with age was found among both men and women.

Figure 1. Percentage of calories from fast food among adults aged 20 and over, by sex and age: United States, 2007–2010

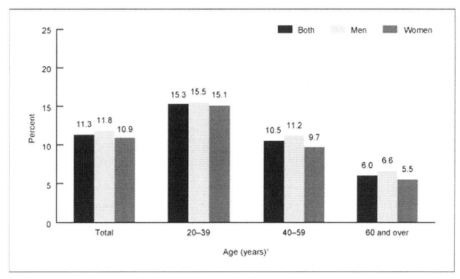

[1]Significant linear trend by age (*p* < 0.05).
NOTE: Total estimates are age adjusted to the 2000 projected U.S. standard population using three age groups: 20–39, 40–59, and 60 and over.
SOURCE: National Health and Nutrition Examination Survey, 2007–2010.

Does the percentage of calories consumed from fast food differ by race and ethnicity?

No significant differences were found between non-Hispanic white and Hispanic adults in the percentage of calories consumed from fast food. The lack of difference, in the percentage of calories consumed from fast food, between non-Hispanic white and Hispanic adults was observed among all age groups. However, among adults aged 20 and over, consumption of calories from fast food was higher among non-Hispanic black adults than non-Hispanic white and Hispanic adults (Figure 2). This disparity was found for young adults aged 20–39, where non-Hispanic black adults consumed more than one-fifth of their percentage of calories from fast food. Among middle-aged adults in the 40–59 age group, the pattern was similar, but the difference between non-Hispanic black and Hispanic persons did not reach statistical significance. No race or ethnic differences were found among adults aged 60 and over.

Figure 2. Percentage of calories from fast food among adults aged 20 and over, by age and race and ethnicity: United States, 2007–2010

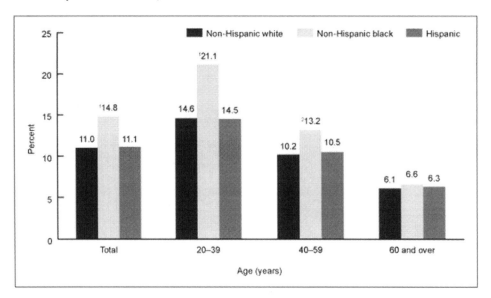

[1]Statistically different from non-Hispanic white and Hispanic adults ($p < 0.05$).
[2]Statistically different from non-Hispanic white adults ($p < 0.05$).
NOTE: Total estimates are age adjusted to the 2000 projected U.S. standard population using three age groups: 20–39, 40–59, and 60 and over.
SOURCE: National Health and Nutrition Examination Survey, 2007–2010.

Does the percentage of calories consumed from fast food differ by income?

Overall, no difference was observed by income status in the percentage of calories consumed from fast food (Figure 3). However, in the youngest age group, 20–39, the percentage of calories consumed from fast food significantly decreased with increasing income level.

Figure 3. Percentage of calories from fast food among adults aged 20 and over, by age and income: United States, 2007–2010

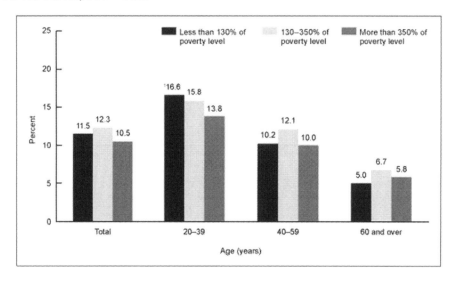

[1]Significant decreasing linear trend ($p < 0.05$).
NOTE: Total estimates are age adjusted to the 2000 projected U.S. standard population using three age groups: 20–39, 40–59, and 60 and over.
SOURCE: National Health and Nutrition Examination Survey, 2007–2010.

Does the percentage of calories consumed from fast food differ by weight status?

Among adults, the percentage of calories consumed from fast food varied by weight status (Figure 4). The percentage of total daily calories from fast food increased as weight status increased. For each age group, obese adults consumed the highest percentage of their calories from fast food.

Figure 4. Percentage of calories from fast food among adults aged 20 and over, by age and weight status: United States, 2007–2010

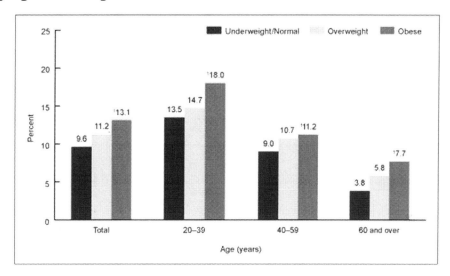

[1]Significant increasing linear trend ($p < 0.05$).
NOTES: Underweight/Normal weight is body mass index (BMI) less than 25.0; overweight is BMI of 25.0–29.9; and obese is BMI greater than or equal to 30.0. Total estimates are age adjusted to the 2000 projected U.S. standard population using three age groups: 20–39, 40–59, and 60 and over.
SOURCE: National Health and Nutrition Examination Survey, 2007–2010.

Summary

An earlier report by the U.S. Department of Agriculture found that the percentage of adults eating fast food increased from the early 1990s to the mid-1990s (1). Moreover, previous studies have reported that more frequent fast-food consumption is associated with higher energy and fat intake and lower intake of healthful nutrients (1,2). This report indicates that for 2007–2010, on average, adults consumed just over one-tenth of their percentage of calories from fast food, which represents a decrease from 2003–2006 when approximately 13% of calories were consumed from fast food.

During 2007–2010, the highest percentage of calories from fast food was consumed among adults who were aged 20–39 or non-Hispanic black or obese. Among young non-Hispanic black adults, more than one-fifth of their calories were consumed from fast food.

From https://www.cdc.gov/nchs/products/databriefs/db114.htm

2. Listen to the following lecture: goo.gl/sfqQv4

3. Prompt: Summarize the points presented in the lecture. Explain how they relate to specific points in the reading passage.

Second Essay

Prepare an essay of about 300–600 words on the topic below.

Some people feel that sharing their lives on social media sites such as Facebook, Instagram, and Snapchat is fine. They share every aspect of their lives, including pictures of themselves and their families, what they ate for lunch, who they are dating, and when they are going on vacation. They even say that if it's not on social media, it didn't happen. Other people believe that sharing so much personal information is an invasion of privacy and could prove dangerous. They think sharing personal pictures and details invites predators, cyberbullying, and identity theft.

Write an essay to someone who is considering whether to participate in social media. Take a side on the issue and argue whether or not he/she should join a social media network. Use specific examples to support your argument.

Dear TOEFL Test Taker,

We would like to start by thanking you for purchasing this study guide for your TOEFL exam. We hope that we exceeded your expectations.

Our goal in creating this study guide was to cover all of the topics that you will see on the test. We also strove to make our practice questions as similar as possible to what you will encounter on test day. With that being said, if you found something that you feel was not up to your standards, please send us an email and let us know.

We would also like to let you know about other books in our catalog that may interest you.

IELTS Study Guide

This can be found on Amazon: amazon.com/dp/162845704X

GRE Study Guide

amazon.com/dp/1628457910

GMAT Study Guide

amazon.com/dp/1628456981

MCAT Study Guide

amazon.com/dp/1628456779

We have study guides in a wide variety of fields. If the one you are looking for isn't listed above, then try searching for it on Amazon or send us an email.

Thanks Again and Happy Testing!
Product Development Team
info@studyguideteam.com

FREE Test Taking Tips DVD Offer

To help us better serve you, we have developed a Test Taking Tips DVD that we would like to give you for FREE. **This DVD covers world-class test taking tips that you can use to be even more successful when you are taking your test.**

All that we ask is that you email us your feedback about your study guide. Please let us know what you thought about it – whether that is good, bad or indifferent.

To get your **FREE Test Taking Tips DVD**, email freedvd@studyguideteam.com with "FREE DVD" in the subject line and the following information in the body of the email:

  a. The title of your study guide.

  b. Your product rating on a scale of 1-5, with 5 being the highest rating.

  c. Your feedback about the study guide. What did you think of it?

  d. Your full name and shipping address to send your free DVD.

If you have any questions or concerns, please don't hesitate to contact us at freedvd@studyguideteam.com.

Thanks again!

Made in the USA
Coppell, TX
17 June 2021